The

Firearm Instructor's Marketing Toolkit

Simple Strategies for Growth and Success

Jim Hankins, USCCA & NRA Instructor

Doreen Hankins, USCCA Instructor & HBIC

Printed by Cloud Bedrock, LLC. in the United States of America.

First printing edition 2024.
Cloud Bedrock, LLC
25986 S. Knollwood Drive
Chesterfield, MI, 48051

Library of Congress Control Number: 2024940875

ISBNs
EPUB: 979-8-9908826-2-1
Kindle: 979-8-9908826-1-4
PDF: 979-8-9908826-3-8
Paperback: 979-8-9908826-0-7
Hardback: 979-8-9908826-4-5

DEDICATION

We dedicate this book to our cat, Mr. Mustache Man.

He did absolutely nothing to assist in the completion of this book.

His appetite for "second breakfast" and his insane desire for us to spend more time at home with him were the catalysts for this project.

We hope he's happy.

CONTENTS

PREFACE

"An idiot with a plan can beat a genius without a plan." — Warren Buffet.

Starting and growing a successful firearm training business requires a blend of expertise, dedication, and savvy business skills. "Build it, and they will come" only works in the movies. Success takes hard work and perseverance.

This guide is designed to help you navigate the complexities of building a thriving firearms training business, from the initial setup to developing some long-term growth strategies.

Whether you are a seasoned firearms trainer or just getting started, this book aims to provide you with the tools and insights needed to build a thriving business.

ACKNOWLEDGEMENTS

Anyone who has ever taken on the task of writing will tell you it's an adventure. Trying to distill your life experiences down into a digestible form that delivers requires benefits from collaboration with others. One indispensable skill set on your team is one of an editor.

A special thanks is owed to Zachary Hankins, who showed endless patience working with Doreen and me as we worked to create this book for all of you.

INTRODUCTION

Who Am I? I like to tell people, "I'm THAT girl".

What does that mean? It depends on who you ask.

My name is Doreen Hankins. I own and operate Detroit Arms, LLC, a firearm training facility just north of Detroit, Michigan, with my husband, Jim Hankins, an NRA and USCCA Instructor.

Detroit Arms began over 16 years ago as a brick-and-mortar gun store/FFL offering the Michigan CPL Class.

If I'm being honest, this was not a career aspiration for me. When Detroit Arms was conceived, I was a "stay at home Mom" who had already had an almost 20-year career in customer service, sales and marketing. No, not McDonalds.

One day, my children (we have four of them) approached their father and said, "PLEASE find something for Mom to do. She's all up in our business at school." I was the overly involved PTO Mom who spent her days volunteering at the school. Every day.

So, doing his due diligence as a dad, Jim approached me and said, "The kids are getting older and need a little more independence. It's time for you to move on to a new phase in life—what do you want to be when you grow up?" I thought about it for a hot minute and then exclaimed, "I think I would like to own a bakery!"

Less than a day later, we inquired about a building just down the street from our house. It was PERFECT—in fact, so perfect that it had been a bakery many years before. How awesome is that?

Fast forward a couple of weeks, and the phone rings at the house. It's the ATF calling to schedule a sight inspection of our new gun store.

"GUN STORE? You have the wrong number." I hang up. They call right back. JIMMMMMMM!!!

It seems that he and the other dads in the neighborhood got to talking, and they collectively decided that a bakery was lame and that it would be WAY cooler to have a gun store. Unbeknownst to me, it was then that Detroit Arms was born.

LONG STORY SHORT

I am not even remotely athletic or tactical. Back then, I did not even own a firearm or know much about them; I would never have claimed to be an enthusiast or even remotely interested. Now, I own a gun store.

There was a learning curve unlike any other. I tried to get "up to speed" on the industry by reading magazines I got from the local bookstore.

Jim, a former Army guy with an NRA Teaching Certificate, hatched a plan to have me run the gun shop during the week, and we would run classes on the weekend.

At the time, Jim's job allowed him to be available to me for questions, etc., so I was confident that I could at least present as a warm body behind the counter.

That was until he heard one-half of a phone conversation.

"Do you sell magazines?" the caller asked. Um, no - I do not sell magazines, but they do sell them at Barnes & Noble. The caller laughed and said, "No, they most certainly do not."

I went on to explain that when you walk in, go about 20 feet in, make a sharp right, and head to the back wall. I was just there last night. They have all the current gun magazines you could ask for!

Jim waited for me to complete the call—the caller wasn't having it—and then asked me to step out from behind the counter - he wanted to show me something. He walked me over to the display wall and proceeded to show me the wide variety of magazines we had for sale.

I had a lot to learn.

It's been a lot of blood, sweat, and tears in the past 16 years. I've even become an instructor myself!

While we can't tell you WHAT to do, we can share with you how we put 20-40 butts in seats each week without utilizing any paid advertising ...using what we call the "Secret Sauce.

"The only place where success comes before work is in the dictionary."
-Vidal Sassoon

1 CHOOSING A NAME, LOGO & BRAND ID

Starting a new business is an exhilarating journey filled with countless decisions that shape its future. Choosing the right name, logo, and brand identity stands out as one of the most crucial steps when you are first getting started.

These elements are not merely aesthetic choices; they encapsulate your business's essence, values, and promise to your customers. Just creating a compelling name and a striking logo can set you apart in a crowded marketplace, while a strong brand identity can foster loyalty and trust from your customers.

Choosing a Name

Reflect on your Business's Nature and Values

- **Relevant and Descriptive:** Ensure your name for your firearm training business relates to the firearm industry. Words like "Arms," "Tactical," "Defense," "Firearms," or "Shooting" can immediately convey the nature of your business. Please keep it simple. Think of words a potential student might instinctively type into a Google search when looking for a firearm trainer. Try to keep numbers out of the name. Acronyms are also difficult for people to digest. Keep it easy to remember.

- **Brand Identity:** Choose a name that aligns with your brand's identity. If you're focusing on tactical and defense markets, terms like "Shield," "Defense," or "Tactical" could be more appropriate than choosing something like your last name or an obscure reference to your favorite movie or superhero.

Ensure Legal Compliance

- **Trademark Search:** Conduct a thorough trademark search to ensure the name you want to use isn't already in use or trademarked. Use resources like the United States Patent and Trademark Office (USPTO) website. https://www.uspto.gov

- **State Regulations:** Some states have naming guidelines for new businesses. Check for state-specific business name regulations and register your company name with the appropriate state authorities.

- **Industry Regulations:** I'm not certain any of these exist, but based on some of the names I've seen in our industry, maybe it's time there were! I've seen some doozies!

Online Presence and Availability

- **Domain Name:** Check the availability of your desired domain name. A matching .com domain is ideal, but other domain name extensions should also be considered if .com is unavailable.

- **Social Media Handles:** Verify the availability of the name on social media platforms – the most commonly used platforms for instructors are Facebook, Twitter, YouTube, TikTok, Instagram.

Marketing Considerations

- **Memorable and Easy to Spell:** Choose a name that is easy to remember, spell, and pronounce. This helps in word-of-mouth marketing and customer recall. REMEMBER SIMPLE!!

- **Avoid Negative Connotations:** Be mindful of the connotations associated with your business name. Avoid names that could be controversial or have negative implications.

- **Look at the Competition:** Look at the names of other firearm training businesses in your area. Don't choose a similar name to avoid brand confusion.

Future Growth and Scalability

- **Broad Appeal:** Choose a name that can grow with your business. Avoid overly specific names that might limit your service range in the future.

- **Market Appeal:** Ensure the name appeals to your target market. For example, suppose you are targeting the basic firearm training market. In that case, the name should resonate with that audience and not sound too "tacticool" which might fend off individuals who are looking for family-friendly or women-friendly training options.

Get Feedback

- **Focus Groups:** Test the name with a diverse range of people— friends, family, potential customers, mentors, and industry peers. This diversity can help ensure the name appeals to a broad audience and doesn't alienate potential customer groups.

- **Surveys:** Consider using social media to survey to understand how a broader audience perceives the name - people LOVE giving their opinions. If the average person in your Facebook friends group is confused by your name - its meaning, spelling, etc. - it stands to reason that the general population will be as well.

Example Names and Considerations

- **Descriptive:** "Precision Firearms," "Elite Tactical Arms"
- **Brand-Oriented:** "Ironclad Defense," "Vanguard Shooting Solutions"
- **Location-Based:** "Texas Tactical Arms," "Midwest Shooting Supplies," "Detroit Arms"
- **Unique and Creative:** "BulletProof Innovations," "ArmorFire Solutions"

Think Long Term

- Envision where you see your business in five or ten years.
- Choose a name that will resonate with your target audience, even as market trends and preferences evolve. Refrain from relying too heavily on current slang or buzzwords that may become outdated or irrelevant.

Choosing A Name Worksheet

Instructions: Use this worksheet to evaluate potential names. For each name, rate the criteria on a scale of 1 to 5 (1 = Poor, 5 = Excellent). Sum the scores to help determine the best choice.

Business Name: _____

Legal Considerations

Trademark Availability: Check if the name is already trademarked.
☐ 1 ☐ 2 ☐ 3 ☐ 4 ☐ 5

Domain Availability: Verify if the domain name is available.
☐ 1 ☐ 2 ☐ 3 ☐ 4 ☐ 5

State Business Name Registration: Confirm the name is available.
☐ 1 ☐ 2 ☐ 3 ☐ 4 ☐ 5

Relevance and Clarity

Descriptive Nature: The name clearly indicates the nature of the business.
☐ 1 ☐ 2 ☐ 3 ☐ 4 ☐ 5

Avoid Misleading Terms: The name is not misleading or too similar to other brands.
☐ 1 ☐ 2 ☐ 3 ☐ 4 ☐ 5

Brand Identity

Target Audience Appeal: The name resonates with the target market.
☐ 1 ☐ 2 ☐ 3 ☐ 4 ☐ 5

Unique and Memorable: The name is distinctive and easy to remember.
☐ 1 ☐ 2 ☐ 3 ☐ 4 ☐ 5

Practicality

Ease of Pronunciation: The name is easy to pronounce.
☐ 1 ☐ 2 ☐ 3 ☐ 4 ☐ 5

Ease of Spelling: The name is easy to spell.
☐ 1 ☐ 2 ☐ 3 ☐ 4 ☐ 5

Intuitive Acronyms: Any acronyms or abbreviations are intuitive.
☐ 1 ☐ 2 ☐ 3 ☐ 4 ☐ 5

Marketing Potential

Logo Compatibility: The name is suitable for logo design.
☐ 1 ☐ 2 ☐ 3 ☐ 4 ☐ 5

Social Media Availability: The name is available on social media platforms.
☐ 1 ☐ 2 ☐ 3 ☐ 4 ☐ 5

Future Expansion

Scalability: The name allows for future growth and diversification.
☐ 1 ☐ 2 ☐ 3 ☐ 4 ☐ 5

Geographic Limitation: The name does not overly limit the business to a specific area.
☐ 1 ☐ 2 ☐ 3 ☐ 4 ☐ 5

Customer Perception

Positive Connotations: The name has positive associations and avoids negative connotations.
☐ 1 ☐ 2 ☐ 3 ☐ 4 ☐ 5

Feedback: Positive feedback from potential customers.
☐ 1 ☐ 2 ☐ 3 ☐ 4 ☐ 5

Cultural Sensitivity

Cultural Appropriateness: The name is appropriate across different cultures.
☐ 1 ☐ 2 ☐ 3 ☐ 4 ☐ 5

Language Appropriateness: The name is appropriate across different languages.
☐ 1 ☐ 2 ☐ 3 ☐ 4 ☐ 5

Avoid Stereotypes: Avoid perpetuating misconceptions that are not only trite but can even be harmful.
☐ 1 ☐ 2 ☐ 3 ☐ 4 ☐ 5

Intellectual Property

Trademark Potential: The name can be trademarked.
☐ 1 ☐ 2 ☐ 3 ☐ 4 ☐ 5

Avoids Infringement: The name does not infringe on existing trademarks.
☐ 1 ☐ 2 ☐ 3 ☐ 4 ☐ 5

Total Score: _____ / 100

Next Steps:

1. Scores: Compare the total scores of each potential name.

2. Select Top Names: Narrow the top 3-5 names based on scores.

3. Final Evaluation: Conduct a final review considering all checklist criteria and additional comments.

4. Decision: Choose the final name and proceed with necessary legal registrations and branding

Using this worksheet, you can systematically evaluate and choose the best name for your firearms business, ensuring it aligns with legal requirements, brand identity, and marketing potential.

If this all sounds like too much, putting your trust in design studios or agencies specializing in brand naming will give you much-needed peace of mind.

There's no shame in hiring a professional to assist in areas you are unsure of - it might save you in the long run.

Logo

Developing a logo for your firearm training business involves several steps to ensure it accurately represents your brand and appeals to your target audience.

Understand Your Brand Identity

- **Define Your Brand:** Clarify your business's mission, values, and unique selling points. Are you focusing on self-defense, competitive shooting, or something else?

- **Target Audience:** Identify your primary audience. Knowing whether you're targeting civilians, law enforcement, military, or recreational shooters will influence the design.

Research and Inspiration

- **Industry Trends:** Look at logos of other firearm training businesses in your market for inspiration. Note what looks good and works well and what doesn't.

- **Visual Elements:** Consider common visual elements in the industry, such as targets, firearms, shields, and crosshairs. Strive to create something unique.

If you look at the Detroit Arms logo, for instance, it is "reminiscent" of the logo of my favorite rock band - Van Halen.

We incorporated that design element with a shield and a firearm to pull the theme together. We used a combination of Jim's favorite colors and mine to pull it all together.

Choose Your Design Elements

- **Symbols and Icons:** Select symbols that represent the essence of your business. Icons like crosshairs, targets, or shields can be effective. You see, we used a hand holding a revolver, which has created some difficulty for us when posting on the internet as some folks are "triggered" by the imagery. It may have been best with just the gun.

- **Typography:** Choose fonts that reflect the tone of your brand. Strong, bold fonts convey power and reliability, while more modern fonts can give a contemporary feel.

- **Colors:** Select a color palette that aligns with the industry and your brand identity. Blue is one of the most common logo colors.

  In fact, one study of 500 company logos found that 37% were blue. Black was a close second at 31%. Blue is a reliable color that conveys positive feelings that many companies would likely want to express, such as trust, security, and intelligence.

  We used Navy blue (Jim's favorite color) and Purple (my favorite color).

- **Imagery:** Decide if you want to incorporate imagery of firearms or related equipment. Ensure the imagery is appropriate and not overly aggressive or controversial.

Design Principles

- **Simplicity:** Aim for a simple and clean design that's easily recognizable and scalable. Complex designs can lose detail when scaled down.

  In our logo, we have some lettering that has proven difficult to remove when embroidering and routinely needs to be removed.

- **Versatility:** Ensure the logo looks good in various sizes and on different materials (e.g., business cards, websites, signage, apparel).

- **Memorability:** Create a design that is distinctive and memorable. A unique logo will stand out and be easier for clients to remember.

Sketch and conceptualize

- **Brainstorming:** Start with rough sketches and multiple concepts. Don't limit your creativity in the initial stages. Computer programs like Canva can be incredibly helpful.

- **Get Feedback:** Share your preliminary designs with friends, family, trusted colleagues, mentors, or even potential customers to get feedback and refine your logo ideas.

Digital Design

- **Design Software:** Use professional design software like Adobe Illustrator or CorelDRAW to create your logo. These tools offer precision and flexibility. Even Canva works!

- **Professional Help:** If you're not confident in your design skills, consider hiring a professional graphic designer. Websites like 99designs, Fiverr, or Upwork can connect you with designers.

Refinement and Testing

- **Revisions:** Be prepared to make several revisions based on feedback. Fine-tune the design until it perfectly represents your brand.

- **Mock-Ups:** Create mock-ups of your logo on different materials and backgrounds to see how it looks in real-world applications.

Finalizing Your Logo

- **File Formats:** Have your logo in various file formats (e.g., PNG, JPG, SVG, AI)

Logo Development Worksheet

Instructions: Use this worksheet to guide the development of your business logo.

Business Name: _____

Logo Development Process:

- **Conceptualization:** Brainstorm and sketch initial ideas.

- **Design Drafts:** Create several design drafts based on the best concepts.

- **Evaluation:** Use this worksheet to evaluate each draft.

- **Feedback:** Gather feedback from stakeholders and potential customers.

- **Refinement:** Refine the design based on feedback and re-evaluate.

- **Finalization:** Choose the final design and create a complete branding

Brand Identity

Reflects Business Values: Does the logo reflect the core values/mission of your business?
☐ 1 ☐ 2 ☐ 3 ☐ 4 ☐ 5

Represents Industry: Does the logo clearly represent the firearms industry?
☐ 1 ☐ 2 ☐ 3 ☐ 4 ☐ 5

Target Audience Appeal: Does the logo resonate with your target market?
☐ 1 ☐ 2 ☐ 3 ☐ 4 ☐ 5

Design Elements

Color Scheme: Are the colors used in the logo appropriate for the brand and industry?
☐ 1 ☐ 2 ☐ 3 ☐ 4 ☐ 5

Typography: Is the font style legible and representative of the brand's personality?

☐ 1 ☐ 2 ☐ 3 ☐ 4 ☐ 5

Iconography: Are the icons or symbols used in the logo relevant and easily recognizable?

☐ 1 ☐ 2 ☐ 3 ☐ 4 ☐ 5

Simplicity and Versatility

Simplicity: Is the logo simple and not overly complicated?

☐ 1 ☐ 2 ☐ 3 ☐ 4 ☐ 5

Versatility: Does the logo work well in various sizes/formats (e.g., print, digital, merch)?

☐ 1 ☐ 2 ☐ 3 ☐ 4 ☐ 5

Scalability: Does the logo maintain clarity and impact when scaled up or down?

☐ 1 ☐ 2 ☐ 3 ☐ 4 ☐ 5

Uniqueness

Distinctiveness: Is the logo unique and easily distinguishable from competitors?

☐ 1 ☐ 2 ☐ 3 ☐ 4 ☐ 5

Memorability: Is the logo memorable and easy to recall?

☐ 1 ☐ 2 ☐ 3 ☐ 4 ☐ 5

Practicality

Reproducibility: Can the logo be easily reproduced in various mediums?

☐ 1 ☐ 2 ☐ 3 ☐ 4 ☐ 5

Cost-Effectiveness: Is the logo cost-effective to print and produce?

☐ 1 ☐ 2 ☐ 3 ☐ 4 ☐ 5

Cultural Sensitivity

Cultural Appropriateness: Is the logo culturally sensitive and appropriate?

☐ 1 ☐ 2 ☐ 3 ☐ 4 ☐ 5

Avoids Negative Connotations: Does the logo avoid negative or unintended connotations?

☐ 1 ☐ 2 ☐ 3 ☐ 4 ☐ 5

Feedback and Testing

Customer Feedback: Have you tested the logo with potential customers for their input?

☐ 1 ☐ 2 ☐ 3 ☐ 4 ☐ 5

Iteration and Improvement: Have you made revisions based on feedback?

☐ 1 ☐ 2 ☐ 3 ☐ 4 ☐ 5

Total Score: _____ / 100

Next Steps:

1. **Scores:** Compare the total scores of each potential name.

2. **Select Top Logo:** Narrow the top 3-5 logos based on scores.

3. **Final Evaluation:** Conduct a final review considering all checklist criteria and additional comments.

4. **Decision:** Choose the final logo and proceed.

Developing a Brand Identity

Developing a brand identity for your firearms training business is a crucial step that can significantly impact both its short-term success and long-term growth.

What is Brand Identity?

Brand identity is the collection of all elements that a company creates to portray the right image to its consumers.

Key Elements of Brand Identity

- **Name and Logo:** These are often the first things a potential customer will notice. Your company name should be memorable and relevant to the services you offer, and the logo should be distinctive and professional.

- **Color Scheme and Typography:** These elements should convey professionalism. Typography has the power to change how people perceive your brand. A well-chosen font can make your brand appear trustworthy, playful, serious, or casual.

- **Messaging and Tone:** The way you communicate with your audience should reflect your values and mission. For a firearms training business, this might include a focus on safety, expertise, and gun owner responsibility.

- **Website and Online Presence:** A well-designed website and active social media profiles can help establish credibility and reach a wider audience. More on this later.

Importance in the Short Term

- **Differentiation:** A strong brand identity helps differentiate your business from competitors. In a crowded market, having a unique and professional appearance can attract customers looking for the best in training services. Detroit Arms, for example, is in a market that literally has instructors on every corner. It wasn't that way when we first started, but it quickly grew as the "getting a concealed pistol license" interest increased. The fact that we went into the market with a well-choreographed image and above-average customer service skills helped set us apart from the casual teachers.

- **First Impressions:** First impressions are crucial. A cohesive and professional brand identity helps make a positive first impression, encouraging potential clients to trust and engage with your business. Remember - You don't get a second chance to make a great first impression. Make sure your brand includes a well thought out and executed measure of exceptional customer service. People will remember how you made them feel long after your interaction with them is over.

- **Marketing and Advertising:** Effective branding makes your marketing efforts more impactful. A recognizable brand can improve the effectiveness of your advertising and promotional activities. The Detroit Arms logo, for example, is often regarded as a "cool image" that our students are proud to display on t-shirts and other merch we have produced in the past.

- **Trust and Credibility:** A consistent brand identity conveys professionalism and reliability, which is essential for building trust with potential clients. Don't go into this all willy-nilly - consistency is key. Pick an image that is not offensive, can grow with you, and will trigger a "Hey, I know them!" response when people see it out in public.

Importance in the Long Term

- **Customer Loyalty and Retention:** A strong brand fosters loyalty. When customers have positive experiences and associate them with your brand, they are more likely to return and refer others. A referred customer costs SIGNIFICANTLY less to obtain than one you have to market to attract. A loyal customer will utilize word of mouth to help you grow.

- **Reputation Building:** Over time, a consistent brand identity helps build a strong reputation. This reputation can lead to word-of-mouth referrals, positive reviews, and a solid standing in the community. We will talk more about Reputation Management later in this guide. It's HUGE.

- **Business Growth:** A recognizable and respected brand can open up new opportunities for growth, such as partnerships, sponsorships, and expansion into new markets or service areas. Build a brand that people are proud to partner with!

- **Higher Perceived Value:** A well-established brand can command higher prices due to the perceived added value. Customers are often willing to pay more for services from a brand they trust and recognize. You've almost certainly never seen a Lamborghini ad on TV, yet they sell cars all over the world at unbelievable prices.

Investing in a strong brand identity for your firearms training business is a strategic move that pays dividends both immediately and over the long haul.

By creating a professional, consistent, and trustworthy brand, you set the foundation for differentiation, trust, and growth. In the competitive firearms training market, a well-crafted brand identity can be a decisive factor in attracting and retaining clients, building a solid reputation, and achieving sustained business success.

Brand Identity Checklist

Research and Analysis
- Conduct thorough market research to help determine your brand.
- Identify and understand your target audience.
- Analyze competitors and market trends.
- Define your company's mission, vision, and core values.
- Establish your unique selling proposition (USP).

Brand Strategy
- Determine brand positioning in the market.
- Develop a clear brand positioning statement.
- Define the brand's personality traits.
- Craft a compelling brand story.

Visual Identity
- Design a distinctive and memorable logo.
- Choose a cohesive color palette that represents your brand.
- Select appropriate typography that reflects your brand's tone.
- Develop a style guide for imagery and other visual elements.

Verbal Identity
- Ensure your brand name is unique and memorable.
- Create a succinct and impactful tagline or slogan.
- Define your brand's voice and tone.

Online Presence

- Design a user-friendly and visually appealing website.
- Establish a consistent brand presence on relevant social media platforms.
- Develop a content strategy that aligns with your brand identity.

Offline Presence

- Create printed materials such as business cards and brochures that reflect your brand.

Legal Considerations

- Register trademarks to protect your brand elements legally.
- Ensure all brand materials comply with relevant laws and regulations.

Usage Instructions:

- Review each item in the checklist and ensure completion.
- Regularly revisit and update the checklist to keep your brand identity relevant and consistent.

Use this checklist as a guide for ongoing brand development and maintenance.

A brand identity is made up of what your brand says, what your values are, how you communicate your product, and what you want people to feel when they interact with your company.

Essentially, your brand identity is the personality of your business and a promise to your customers.

If you follow the components of brand identity - verbal, visual, and emotional - you've taken the first step towards building a strong brand that resonates with your dream clients to build loyalty, helps you stand out from the competition, and attracts new customers/clients.

"Whether you think you can or you think you can't—you're right."
- Henry Ford

2 SETTING UP YOUR BUSINESS

The goal of this book is not to give legal or state specific rules and regulations about becoming a firearms instructor, but rather provide you a roadmap for making the business you create a successful venture.

Each state has their own set of rules and regulations for what constitutes a lawful business and it's on YOU as a business owner to know what they are and abide by them.

On a high level, before you go down the path of announcing yourself to the world as a trainer, there are a number of considerations you should review.

Setting Up Your Business

• **Legal Considerations:** Decide whether to register as an LLC, corporation, or sole proprietorship. When deciding between a single-member LLC and a sole proprietorship, focus on the needs of your business.

As an entrepreneur testing the waters, a sole proprietorship may be an easy and cost-effective option, while a fast-growing business that needs funding would be better suited to an LLC. You can find detailed explanations on sites such as https://www.legalzoom.com.

• **Permits:** Obtain all necessary federal, state, and local licenses. If you plan on selling firearms to your students, an FFL License will be necessary.

Your state or local government may require that you obtain a business license or special permitting to host classes, even in your own home. Do your due diligence and make sure you operate within the confines of the law.

• **Certifications:** Receive the appropriate Certifications to teach in your state. Each state has different requirements to become a Concealed Carry Instructor. Hopefully you checked into which discipline they accept (USCCA, NRA, etc.) prior to obtaining your instructor certification.

Do you grab all the certifications you can or pick them up as you go?

Only you, your wallet, the time you have to invest, and your market demand can answer that question. There's no easy answer to this because we, as instructors, should always be training. Know your core strengths and teach based on those.

• **Insurance:** Secure appropriate insurance coverage to protect your business and clients. Firearms instructors need to remain vigilant, protecting themselves against risk from all accidents, including injury, damage, negligence, and even fatality.

• **Finding a Location:** This is EASILY one of the most difficult tasks for any new instructor.

You should first, and foremost, consider the comfort level of your students when making this decision. Remember, not everyone is comfortable coming to the home of an instructor to complete their training.

Likewise, offering to provide the classroom portion of training in THEIR home makes scaling your training business difficult. It's easy to find options for a working classroom without getting locked into a lease on a building.

- Public Libraries
- Civic Buildings/Community Centers
- Churches/Religious Institutions
- Cafés and Restaurants
- Parks & Recreation Areas
- Non-Profit Organizations
- Local Businesses Conference Rooms
- Colleges & Universities
- Apartment Complex Clubhouses
- YMCA or Recreational Facilities
- Maker Spaces/Innovation Hubs
- Union Halls
- Commercial Training Centers
- Conference Rooms in Hotels

The most daunting task for most is finding a range to utilize for the shooting portion of any training.

While there are typically both indoor and outdoor ranges in nearly every marketplace, not every range is open to allowing instructors to shoot with students.

There can be several reasons why a gun range might not allow an instructor to train their students at their facility for live fire. Some of these reasons include:

- **Liability and Insurance Concerns:** Gun ranges have strict insurance policies and liability concerns. If an external instructor is not covered under the range's insurance or has not provided proof of their own insurance, the range might not allow them to instruct to avoid any potential legal and financial risks in case of an accident.

- **Range Safety and Protocols:** Each gun range has its own safety protocols and rules. An external instructor might not be familiar with these specific protocols, which could lead to safety breaches. The range management might want to ensure that all instructions are in line with their established safety procedure if they do consider you for training.

- **Instructor Credentials and Qualifications:** The range might have concerns about the credentials or qualifications of the instructor. They may have a vetting process to ensure that any instructor teaching on their premises meets their standards and has all of the necessary certifications required in your city or state.

- **Range Policies and Agreements:** Some ranges have policies that only allow their in-house instructors to conduct training. This could be part of their business model to ensure consistent quality of instruction and to generate revenue through their staff.

- **Previous Incidents:** If the range itself or a particular instructor has had previous incidents or complaints at the range or other ranges, the management might decide not to allow them to instruct on their premises.

- **Conflicts of Interest:** If the instructor is affiliated with a competing range or business, the range might see this as a conflict of interest and deny access to protect their business interests.

- **Range Capacity and Scheduling:** The range might have limited space and time slots available, and giving priority to their instructors ensures that their resources are used efficiently. External instructors might disrupt their scheduling and resource allocation.

- **Membership and Affiliation Requirements:** Some ranges may have specific requirements for instructors to be members or affiliated with certain organizations or associations before they can teach there.

To resolve such issues, the instructor can always opt to directly communicate with the range management in order to understand their specific concerns and requirements.

Providing proof of insurance, demonstrating familiarity with the range's safety protocols, and showing credentials and references can help address the range's concerns and potentially allow the instructor to conduct training sessions.

You might even consider "helping out" free of charge at the range to establish a rapport with the staff before asking to train your students there. Let them get familiar with you, your style, and the fact that you can be trusted to be safe in their facility.

• **Equipment and Supplies:** Investing in the right equipment is crucial. Maintaining a variety of firearms for training purposes, eye and ear protection, first aid kits, training aids such as dummy rounds, targets, and simulation equipment to enhance the learning experience can get expensive QUICK. Pace   yourself.

These things add up quickly, and you may find yourself with a bunch of tools that don't work for the classes that end up being most popular in your community.

"Start where you are. Use what you have. Do what you can."
- Arthur Ashe

3 WEBSITE 101

Setting up a website. Seems simple enough, right? I've seen instructors who have tackled it themselves. I've seen instructors who have out-tasked it to friends and family. I've seen instructors who have hired it out to a third party. There's really no right answer.

I can also tell you HORROR stories for each instance. There's more than meets the eye when building a website for your brand, and if you are not familiar with what goes on behind the curtain. BUYER BEWARE.

Some instructors never put up a website of their own but rather rely on third-party booking apps or the sites provided to them as instructors for their brand. This is not a great idea either - you need to **OWN YOUR OWN BRAND**. More on this later.

Website 101

As a firearms instructor, having a professional online presence is essential for attracting clients, showcasing your expertise, and providing critical information about your services.

IT'S YOUR 24-HOUR-A-DAY, 7-DAY-A-WEEK, 365-DAY-A-YEAR SALESPERSON FOR YOUR BUSINESS!

When it comes to developing a website, you face a significant decision: should you self-publish or hire a professional web developer?

Each approach has its advantages and challenges, and understanding them will help you make an informed choice that aligns with your business goals and resources.

Self-Publishing Your Website - $100 - $1,000

Pros:

- **Cost-Effective: One** of the primary advantages of self-publishing your website is the potential cost savings. Website builders like Wix, Squarespace, and WordPress offer affordable plans that include hosting, domain names, and a variety of templates. These platforms are user-friendly, even for those with minimal technical skills.

- **Control and Flexibility:** Building your own website allows you to have full control over the design, content, and updates. You can make changes on the fly without waiting for a developer's availability, ensuring that your site remains current and relevant.

- **Learning Experience:** Developing your own website can be a valuable learning experience. You'll gain new skills in website design, SEO (Search Engine Optimization), and digital marketing, which can be beneficial for your business in the long run.

Cons:

- **Time-Consuming:** Building and maintaining a website takes time, which might detract from your core activities of instructing and managing your business.

  The initial setup and ongoing maintenance can be particularly time-intensive if you are not familiar with web design principles.

  Personally, as an instructor, I want to focus on income-producing activities, not learning a new computer program or worrying about the design elements of a good website.

  Hiring a friend or family member might not be the best option either. We all know someone who can "Get us a hook-up" but, in the end, such deals don't always fair well.

  I recently worked with an instructor who had a friend set up his website as a favor.

  When the friendship ended, he found out that his former friend not only owned his domain name (because he registered it), but he also had complete control of his business website.

- **Limited Customization:** While website builders are convenient, they can also be limiting. You might find yourself constrained by the templates and functionalities available, which could impact the uniqueness and professionalism of your website.

  The reality here is that more is not always better. A simple website is better than no website. There are some "overthought" websites out there that are hard to navigate and provide little benefit to the instructor or the potential client.

- **Technical Challenges:** Although website builders are designed to be user-friendly, you may still encounter technical challenges. Handling issues related to site security, performance, and complex design elements can be daunting without technical expertise. Oh, and technical support is not typically free. It's a bonus.

Hiring a Professional Web Developer - $500 - $50,000

Pros:

- **Professional Quality:** A professional web developer can create a highly polished, custom website that truly reflects your brand and stands out in a competitive market.

- **Time Savings:** Hiring a professional allows you to focus on your business while the developer handles the website creation. Time is money.

- **Ongoing Support:** Many web developers offer ongoing maintenance and support services. This means you have an expert on hand to handle updates, troubleshoot issues, and keep your website running smoothly.

Cons:

- **Higher Cost:** Professional web development can be expensive, with initial setup costs and potential ongoing fees for maintenance and updates. This investment might be challenging for small businesses or startups with limited budgets. There are also other considerations like SEO, getting locked into a hosting plan, etc. to consider.

- **Dependency on Developer:** Relying on a web developer means you might face delays when you need changes or updates. This dependency can be frustrating if the developer is not immediately available or you can't afford to hire them for any more hours.

- **Communication Challenges:** Effectively communicating your vision and requirements to a developer can sometimes be challenging. The firearms training industry is a niche market with specific needs. Misunderstandings or miscommunications can result in a website that does not fully meet your expectations or costs more than planned.

Alternative Options - $0 - $10,000/year

- **Go Without:** NOT an optimal choice if we are being honest. We are building a brand. Having a website allows you to build credibility with your potential customers and clients, giving them confidence that they're engaging with a professional company.

- **Link to a 3rd Party Source:** There are Marketplace options out there that will allow you to create an instructor profile and landing page for your business that you can then utilize as a website alternative. NOT replacement - an alternative.

The USCCA, for example, has such a benefit. It's free for USCCA instructors to use, and it allows USCCA instructors to list their classes and link student registration and payment to your Stripe account. This is a cost-effective option for many instructors but not a be-all-end-all. There are limitations to utilizing this option that we will cover later.

Other paid-for platforms offer robust options for instructors that include the ability to have a profile and landing page, as well as a wide array of other business-enhancing tools. It's a pay-to-play scenario where you either give up a portion of the proceeds from each student booking fee to participate or pay a set monthly fee.

These platforms also allow potential clients to view classes offered by all of the participating instructors in a particular search area, which puts your offerings up against other instructors in your market. We want the focus to be on YOU and YOUR classes.

These marketplaces also tend to have some control measures designed to make you dependent on their platform for marketing and collecting student reviews, which are HUGE to your success. More on this in the Google Business Profile section.

Key Factors in Making the Decision

- **Budget:** Assess your financial resources. If funds are tight, self-publishing might be the better option. If you can afford it, investing in a professional website might pay off.

- **Time:** Consider how much time you can realistically dedicate to building and maintaining a website. If your schedule is already packed, hiring a professional might save you valuable time and energy.

- **Skills and Interest:** Reflect on your technical skills and interest in web design. If you enjoy learning new things and are confident in your ability to manage a website, self-publishing could be rewarding. Conversely, if you prefer to focus on your core business activities, a professional developer might be more suitable.

- **Business Goals:** Think about your long-term business goals. A professionally developed website can enhance your brand's credibility and potentially attract more clients. However, a well-designed self-published website can also achieve these goals if executed properly.

I highly encourage you to make having a website a priority for your firearm training business. Dollar for dollar is a cost-effective way to showcase your talents and offerings, build your brand, boost brand awareness, build credibility, and grow your firearm training business.

It's a platform that you can build upon to enhance your training offerings to your students. Detroit Arms, for example, offers our traditional in-person training AND an ever-growing list of Video on Demand classes available 24 hours a day, seven days a week, 365 days a year. No dependency on a classroom, weather or schedules - we literally make money while we sleep.

How WE handle it...

As small business owners, we've bootstrapped all the expenses for the launch and development of Detroit Arms. As you can imagine, it was never desirable to put up collateral such as our home to secure the financing to go "all out" with branding, marketing, etc.

While we believed in ourselves and our product, we also thought it important to ensure we had a home at the end of the day if our vision was off.

That meant we took on the task of building **EVERYTHING**, including our website, independently. There was no budget to hire some fancy, schmancy firm to create an image and write the vocabulary. Just me, my grasp of the English language, and what I knew about marketing.

Jim is a technology wizard. Literally. Me, not so much. I've made several websites in my day, but none were developed and launched without his technological prowess in the background, bringing them to life. I would not have taken it on if I didn't have him behind me.

If you visit our website (www.DetroitArms.com) you will see it is what some may consider "incredibly basic". Just the facts. No glitter or glam - no bells and whistles - no chest-thumping about how great we are.

This is just the information people are looking for when they are seeking firearm training. To say it has served us well is an understatement. It is everything we need it to be.

If you struggle with things like the lack of a website, or maybe the website you have is not delivering to your expectations, or maybe you need help in general marketing your business, we will dive more into how you can find affordable and knowledgeable assistance.

Hint: It's me - I'm the one - I can help you. Keep reading.

Your Website and Brand Control

Maintaining ownership of your brand is crucial for any small business owner because your brand is your identity in the marketplace.

It encompasses everything from your logo and slogan to the overall perception customers have of your business. One of the most critical aspects of brand ownership in the digital age is controlling your website.

If you read nothing else in this chapter - THIS IS WHAT YOU NEED TO KNOW.

We work with instructors nationwide and repeatedly run into the same scenario.

THEY DON'T OWN THEIR BRAND.

They allow others to control it for them. **BIG MISTAKE.**

How does that happen, you wonder?

There are dozens of ways. They have someone else purchase a domain name for them off GoDaddy rather than making their own account. They let someone else maintain creative control over their website without maintaining administrative access for themselves.

They don't set up a website - they rely on a 3rd party site for their "page," and that site controls all the information your customer sees AND all of the customer feedback, aka. **REVIEWS THAT YOU NEED** for the betterment of your business on your Google Business Profile.

You will read all about that in the next chapter. And yes, it's that important. **YOU NEED TO MAINTAIN CONTROL OF YOUR BRAND.** It's ok to rely on others for assistance, but you need to control it at the end of the day.

Website Ownership

Domain Name Control

- **Ownership of the Domain:** The domain name (e.g., yourbusiness.com) is your online address and a significant part of your brand identity. If you let someone else register the domain on your behalf without transferring ownership to you, they technically own that address. This could lead to complications if the relationship soured or the person/company went out of business.

- **Implications of Losing the Domain:** If you don't own your domain, you risk losing it if the person controlling it decides to sell it, abandon it, or if you have a disagreement. Reacquiring a domain can be costly and time-consuming, potentially resulting in a loss of customer trust and brand consistency.

Content Control

- Complete Access and Editing Rights: When someone else builds your website, it's crucial that you have full administrative access. This means you can update, modify, and manage the content independently. Without this control, you may face delays or extra costs every time you need a change or update.

- **Content Ownership:** All content on the website (text, images, videos, blogs, etc.) should be owned by you. If the developer retains rights to the content, they can remove it or restrict your use, causing significant disruptions to your business operations.

Importance of Ownership

Consistency and Branding

- Maintaining control ensures that your brand message stays consistent. If you need to quickly adapt your messaging or update your branding elements, you can do so without waiting for a third party.

- Consistent branding across all platforms helps in building customer trust and loyalty.

Security and Reliability

- Having control over your domain and content reduces the risk of cyber threats. If you manage the domain and hosting, you can implement and oversee security measures directly.

- Reliance on a third party for critical aspects of your online presence can introduce risks. If their service is interrupted, it directly impacts your website's availability.

Flexibility and Scalability

- Owning your domain and having full control over your website allows you to scale and expand your online presence as needed. You can add new features, integrate with other services, and make significant changes without being held back by a third party.

Financial Control

- Managing your own domain and content can be more cost-effective in the long run. You can avoid potential markup costs and fees associated with using a third-party for management of your website and domain.

- Ownership avoids unexpected costs associated with transferring ownership or resolving disputes over your website and domain.

Best Practices

- **Register the Domain Yourself:** Always register the domain name personally or ensure that it is registered under your name and business, not the developer's. OWN YOUR OWN DOMAIN!!!

  Keep an eye on that expiration date, or you will lose access to your domain!

- **Full Administrative Access**: Ensure you have full administrative access to your website's content management system (CMS) and hosting platform.

- **Consider Getting Your Own Hosting Plan:** By managing your own hosting, you have a clear understanding of the costs involved and can choose a plan that fits your budget without hidden fees.

  Third-party developers or agencies may charge a premium for hosting services. Managing your own hosting can be more cost-effective in the long run.

- **Clear Contracts:** When hiring someone to create your website, have a clear contract that specifies your ownership of the domain and all content, written and photos, as well as administrative access rights.

  Make sure YOU maintain control at all costs.

- **Regular Backups:** Regularly back up your website to ensure that you have a copy of your content and data that you can restore independently if needed. It is traditionally not the responsibility of the third-party website developer to do this for you.

  With your own hosting platform, you can regularly back up your website data and ensure you have copies stored securely.

By maintaining ownership of your domain and control over your website content, you safeguard your brand's integrity, ensure operational flexibility, and protect your business from potential risks and dependencies on third parties.

Website Development Worksheet

Planning and Preparation

- Define Goals and Objectives
- Determine what you want your website to achieve (e.g., attract new clients, provide training resources, feature a class schedule, sell merchandise).
- Identify your target audience.
- Market Research
- Analyze competitors' websites.
- Identify the unique selling points (USPs) of your business.
- Content Planning
- List the main pages you need (e.g., Home, About, Classes, Contact)
- Outline the content for each page.
- Plan for any multimedia content (videos, images, downloadable PDFs).

Domain and Hosting

- Choose a Domain Name - Ideally, it should be your actual business name.
- A .com name is preferred but not necessary.
- Ensure it is easy to remember and type.
- Make sure **YOU OWN** the domain name and not a 3rd party.
- Select a Hosting Provider
- Look for reliability, speed, and good customer support.
- Consider the scalability and specific needs of your website, both currently and what you need for the future (e.g., e-commerce, booking system).
- Make sure **YOU** hold **ALL** the access credentials needed to update/make changes, and that these permissions are held by a 3rd party.

Design and Development

- Choose a clean, professional design that reflects your brand.
- Ensure the design is mobile-responsive as most viewers will be viewing your website on a cellphone and not on a desktop computer.
- Create a mockup of your site and what you expect it to look like.
- Consider your colors - both for regular and dark mode viewing.
- Keep it simple - don't force viewers to scroll the entire site on your schedule.
- Choose a platform (e.g., WordPress, Wix, Squarespace).
- Set up and customize your chosen theme/template if self-publishing.
- Integrate necessary plugins (e.g., SEO tools, security, analytics).
- Create high-quality content - Write engaging and informative content for each page. Not a word salad; remember, more is not always better. Stay focused and to the point.
- Include keywords for SEO (Search Engine Optimization).
- Create or source high-quality images and videos - a picture is worth a thousand words! Students often like to see photos of you, your facility/classroom, the range, and any other visuals that would make choosing you a no-brainer. Don't make the site TOO TACTICOOL, as this may drive off the casual gun enthusiast.
- Legal and Safety Information - Include any disclaimers, cancellation/rescheduling policies, safety guidelines, Terms of Service, Privacy Policy, and refund policy you may have.
- Ensure content complies with all local and national regulations.

Functional Elements

- Booking and Scheduling System - Will you need a system for clients to book courses or sessions online?
- Ensure it is user-friendly and integrates with your calendar.
- E-Commerce Functionality - How are your students going to PAY for your services?
- Are you planning on selling products as well as services?
- Ensure secure payment processing.
- Contact and Communication - Include an easy-to-use contact form.

- Provide clear contact information (email, phone number, physical address).
- Integrate a live chat feature if possible. **THIS IS HUGE!!** I book students using the chat feature **DAILY**. Chat can be added to your website, social media and more - do NOT sleep on this option.

SEO and Analytics

- SEO Optimization - Optimize all content for search engines.
- Use relevant keywords, meta tags, and alt text for images.
- Create a sitemap and submit it to search engines.
- Analytics Setup - Integrate Google Analytics or other tracking tools.
- Set up goals and track conversions.

IT SHOULD BE NOTED - SEO Optimization can be a pricey upsell and is not always the fastest way to get your information noticed on the internet. Speed to market and the ability to be found by customers are enhanced by your Google Business Profile, which we will discuss later.

Testing and Launch
- Pre-Launch Testing - Test website functionality on different browsers and internet-connected devices.
- Check for broken links and errors.
- Ensure all forms and interactive elements work correctly.

Launch the Website
- Announce the launch on social media and via email to any existing clients.

Post-Launch
- Monitor Performance
- Regularly check website analytics.
- Monitor user feedback and reviews.
- Update Content - Keep the website updated with new content, blog posts, and course information. Regularly refresh multimedia content.
- Maintenance - Perform regular backups. Your web host might not provide this automatically.
- Update plugins and software.
- Ensure the website remains secure.

"Setting goals is the first step in turning the invisible into the visible." — Tony Robbins

4 CREATING A CURRICULUM AND TRAINING PROGRAMS

Creating a comprehensive curriculum and training programs as a firearms instructor requires careful planning and adherence to safety, legal, and educational standards.

Each state has its own set of rules and regulations for what constitutes an appropriate training program to receive any type of state-issued firearm license, and it's on YOU as a firearms instructor to know what they are and abide by them.

Likewise, the state you reside in will likely require that you are certified by or hold credentials from a nationally recognized organization, such as the United States Concealed Carry Association (USCCA) or the National Rifle Association (NRA).

Creating a Curriculum and Training Programs

Developing a comprehensive curriculum and training program as a firearms instructor necessitates meticulous planning and compliance with safety, legal, state, and educational standards.

In addition to the curriculums provided by your certifying organization, you have the flexibility to create your own classes.

Remember – If you can think it, you can teach it!

Define Objectives and Goals

- **Skill Levels:** Determine the skill levels you will address (e.g., beginner, intermediate, advanced).

- **Learning Outcomes**: Specify what students should know and be able to do by the end of the course.

- **Safety Standards:** Emphasize safety as a primary objective in all training activities.

Legal and Ethical Considerations

- **Compliance:** Ensure all training materials and activities comply with local, state, and federal laws.

- **Ethical Standards:** Maintain high ethical standards, making sure to include all facets of responsible gun ownership and usage.

Curriculum Structure

- **Course Syllabus:** Outline the topics covered, including safety, maintenance, marksmanship, and situational training.

- **Modules and Sessions:** Break down the curriculum into manageable modules and sessions.

Instructional Methods

- **Teaching Techniques:** Use a mix of lectures, demonstrations, student involvement, and hands-on practice to keep student engagement in check.

- **Learning Styles:** Cater to various learning styles (visual, auditory, kinesthetic, reading/writing) to ensure comprehensive understanding from all students.

- **Training Platforms:** Not every class needs to be in a classroom - virtual learning is hot.

Basic Safety Training

- **Introduction to Firearms:** Covering the basics of different types of firearms, their parts, and how they operate. Include a section on verbiage used - it makes taking a class easier if you understand the language.

- **Fundamentals of Firearm Safety:** Cover key safety rules for ownership, transportation, use, safe muzzle direction, trigger discipline, safe storage, and more.

- **Emergency Procedures:** Teach emergency response procedures, which might include basic first aid, bleeding control, active threat assessment, and handling gun malfunctions.

Firearms Basics

- **Types of Firearms:** Explain different types of firearms (handguns, rifles, shotguns).

- **Handgun Basics:** Focusing on proper grip, stance, sight alignment, and trigger control for handguns.

- **Rifle Basics:** Covering the fundamentals of rifle shooting, including proper posture, aiming, and shooting techniques.

- **Shotgun Basics:** Teaching the essentials of shotgun use, including mounting, aiming, and shooting at stationary and moving targets.

- **Ammunition:** Educate about various types of ammunition and their characteristics.

- **Firearm Mechanics:** Describe the parts of a firearm and their functions.

Marksmanship and Shooting Techniques

- **Intermediate Handgun Techniques:** Building on basic skills with advanced grip, stance, and movement techniques.

- **Aiming and Trigger Control:** Focus on sight alignment, sight picture, and trigger pull.

- **Breathing and Follow-through:** Emphasize the importance of breathing control and follow-through after each shot.

- **Advanced Rifle Marksmanship:** Covering long-distance shooting, windage and elevation adjustments, and shooting positions.

- **Tactical Shotgun Training:** Teaching defensive shotgun techniques, including reloading under pressure and target transitions.

- **Dry Fire Techniques:** A cost-effective way to improve shooting skills is by focusing on techniques without distractions. Helps develop muscle memory and enhances trigger control.

Practical Application

- **Actual Range Time:** Live-fire practice on a range under supervision.

- **Scenario-based Training:** Use real-life scenarios to teach decision-making and situational awareness. If you don't have access to a series of videos that cover this topic, just scan YouTube for ideas.

- **Shooting Simulators** - Safe, economical situation training without real bullets.

- **Laser Training** - There's a wide variety of interactive laser training options available for both in-home and in-classroom use that are safe, inexpensive and practical. We have both SIRT pistols and the less expensive LaserLyte guns in our classroom.

Specialty Courses

- **Women's Only Classes:** Tailored to address the unique concerns and preferences of female shooters, creating a comfortable learning environment.

- **Youth Firearm Safety and Training:** Teaching children and teenagers the basics of firearm safety and shooting in a controlled and safe manner.

- **Real Estate Agent Safety:** Real estate agents have safety concerns due to the nature of their job. They often work alone, in unfamiliar surroundings with unfamiliar people.

- **Home Defense:** Teaching strategies for protecting oneself and family within the home, including firearm selection and safe room tactics.

- **Travel Safety:** We can't take our firearms everywhere, so teach strategies for protecting oneself and family while traveling by utilizing situational awareness, de-escalation techniques, and weapons of opportunity.

- **Senior Citizen Safety:** How to avoid potentially harmful situations and proven techniques that do not rely on physical contact or weapons for the elderly individual who cannot or does not want to undertake demanding self-defense training but wants the self-confidence of knowing what to do in a bad situation.

- **School Campus Safety:** Many college campuses do not allow guns or pepper spray, so arm students with proven safety techniques to use while on campus.

Certified Specialized Training

- Concealed Carry Classes: Educating on the legal and practical aspects of carrying a concealed firearm, including situational awareness and holster selection.

Thinking Outside the Box

"I have a very particular set of skills." Liam Neeson

A quote from the movie Taken. **YOU TOO** have skills that you may have acquired over a very long career, or skills you recently acquired that would come in handy to someone in your community.

Skills that can earn your income, increase class interest and size, and allow you to showcase the need for better-prepared human beings.

Some classes should only be taught in person. You can't argue that.

However, there's a plethora of information YOU CAN TEACH that doesn't require a classroom, doesn't require a schedule (because it's recorded), doesn't require the use of a range, AND can widen your customer base from what would normally be about a 50-mile radius to anywhere in the world.

What if I told you you could create **YOUR OWN** content that can be delivered 24 hours a day, seven days a week, 365 days a year to anyone **ANYWHERE IN THE WORLD:**

- Basic Firearm Safety
- Situational Awareness Skills
- Reasons Why... <Insert ANY Safety Related Topic Here>
- Basic Self-Defense Techniques
- Utilizing Weapons of Opportunity
- Developing a Safety Plan for Your Home - You - Kids - Your Family
- Senior Citizen Safety
- College Campus Safety
- Travel Safety

THE LIST IS ENDLESS, and you are only restrained by your knowledge and creativity. We will talk more about HOW you can do this later.

"The best way to do it is to do it."
— Amelia Earhart

5 MARKETING YOUR TRAINING BUSINESS

Starting a firearm training business is just the beginning; effectively marketing it is crucial for attracting and retaining clients. With the right strategies, you can distinguish your business in a competitive market.

We've already discussed the cornerstones of getting your business ready for market. We've covered choosing a name, determining your brand identity and why it is important, and the ins and outs of creating a logo and website. We even put together some ideas for training.

There are DOZENS of ways to get the word out, both paid and unpaid. If we are being honest, most new instructors are ballers on a budget - this business does not come cheap. Let's talk about basic marketing.

Networking and Building Professional Relationships

Networking is an invaluable aspect of marketing your firearm training business. Stepping out of your comfort zone with friends and family is key. By building relationships with other professionals in your area, you can open doors to new opportunities and gain referrals.

Join both industry-specific and non-industry-related related associations and groups in your area. These organizations often host events that provide platforms for connecting with peers.

- **Visit Local Gun Shops:** Get to know the owner. Offer to refer students to them for their firearm needs in exchange for leaving your business cards or class brochures behind.

- **Outdoor and Hunting Stores:** Collaborate with stores that cater to outdoor enthusiasts and hunters. Get to know the people behind the gun counter. You'd be surprised at how often they get asked for assistance in finding a trainer or a class.

- **Local Gun Clubs and Shooting Ranges:** Engage with members and offer to conduct or assist in conducting training sessions or safety seminars.

- **Partner With Other Instructors:** There's no shame in presenting a united front. Offer to co-teach a class or offer your services as a range safety officer for one of their classes. This is a great opportunity for you to learn from a more seasoned instructor who might consider taking you under their wing.

- **Join your local Chamber of Commerce:** Being part of a chamber is a great way to get to know businesses and business owners in your community. Your new business friends will probably be happy to support you with discounts, advice, assistance with special tasks, word-of-mouth marketing, collaborative projects, and more.

- **Join Other Business Networking Groups:** Connect with the US Small Business Association (SBA), join a Business Networking International (BNI) group, or use MeetUp.com.

- **Community Events:** Attend gun shows, fairs, and community events to increase visibility. Many local community farmers markets allow local business owners to rent a space to promote their business. Arts and crafts show sell booth space as well.

- **Safety Seminars:** Conduct gun safety seminars at schools, community centers, and clubs to educate and promote your services.

- **Consultation Sessions:** Provide free initial consultations to local businesses. Real Estate agents are a prime market for us as trainers. They have safety concerns that we can address as trainers. Ask to be invited to their weekly sales meeting to introduce yourself. This gives them a taste of your expertise and encourages them to sign up for training.

- **Gun Owners of America (GOA):** https://gunowners.org

- **National Rifle Association (NRA):** https://nra.org

- **United States Practical Shooting Association:** https://uspsa.org

"You don't get referrals for doing your job. You get referrals for doing everything else." - Alex Hormozi.

"They can't HIRE you if they can't FIND you."— Me, Doreen Hankins.

6 GOOGLE BUSINESS PROFILE

A Google Business Profile (GBP) is a free, powerful tool provided by Google that allows businesses to manage their online presence across Google's vast ecosystem, including Search and Maps.

It serves as a central hub for your business's information, ensuring that potential customers can easily find and interact with your business online. If you do nothing else to promote your business - **DO THIS**. Your GBP is **GOLD.**

By leveraging a Google Business Profile effectively, you can significantly enhance your business's online presence, attract more local customers, and build a strong online reputation.

It is **NOT ENOUGH** to just get listed on Google.

You need to work diligently to ensure your listing contains all the key elements of a **GREAT** listing; relevant keywords, proper location and service information, business hours, photos, interaction, etc. and we are going to walk you through that, step-by-step.

Benefits of Google Business Profile

Enhanced Visibility:

- **Search Engine Optimization (SEO):** A fully optimized GBP helps improve your local SEO, making your business more visible in local search results and Google Maps.

  It should be noted that you can spend hundreds, even thousands, of dollars on SEO for your website and then be forced to wait 6 months for results or you can get **FREE,** nearly **IMMEDIATE**, results with a Google Business Profile. It's that good.

- **Google Maps Integration:** Ensures your business appears on Google Maps, which is crucial for local businesses. You can be listed even if you don't have a brick-and-mortar business.

Increased Trust and Credibility:

- **Verified Listings:** Google's verification adds legitimacy and trustworthiness to your business.

- **Customer Reviews:** Positive reviews enhance your credibility and attract more customers. Even a bad review can be used to your advantage if you respond properly. We all know there are THREE sides to every story...

Customer Engagement and Interaction:

- **Customer Engagement:** It provides a platform for engaging with customers through reviews, Q&A, and posts about updates, promotions, and events. It should be noted that Google has announced the end of Chat on July 31, 2024.

- **Feedback and Reviews:** Allows you to respond to reviews, showing that you value customer feedback and are committed to improving your services.

Setting up your Google Business Profile is EASY!

- Sign in to Google My Business:
- Go to Google My Business.
- Click on "Manage now."
- Sign in with your Google account. If you don't have one, you'll need to create one.

Enter Your Business Name

Type in your business name. If it doesn't appear in the drop-down menu, click on "Add your business to Google."

Choose Your Business Category

Select the category that best fits your business. This helps Google show your business in relevant search results. We choose Firearms Academy.

Add Your Location

If you have a physical location where customers can visit, enter your address. If you operate a service-area business (meaning you do NOT have a set location that you teach in), select that option and specify the area you serve.

Enter Contact Details

Add your phone number and website URL so customers can reach you easily.

Verify Your Business

Google will require verification to confirm that you are the owner of the business. Verification methods include postcard by mail, phone, email, or instant verification (if you've already verified your website with Google Search Console).

Complete Your Profile

Once verified, complete your profile by adding business hours, photos, a business description, and any other relevant information. Make sure to keep your information up to date.

Optimize Your Profile

Regularly update your profile with posts about promotions, events, and new products or services. Encourage satisfied customers to leave positive reviews.

Tips for Maximizing Your Google Business Profile

A correctly optimized Google Business Profile significantly influences your ranking. Google's algorithm pays attention to the content of your listing (relevant keywords), activity with your customers, and the completeness of your listing and rewards you for it by ranking you higher!

- **Ask For and Respond to Reviews:** Engage with your customers by asking for reviews and then responding to their reviews, showing that you value their feedback.

- **Business Hours:** Google has updated its ranking algorithm in the Maps area to place more emphasis on hours of operation. When someone searches on Google, businesses listed as "open" at that exact moment will have the best chance of ranking in the top three results.

- **Use High-Quality Images:** Upload high-resolution images that showcase your business, products, or services. Hint: People LOVE to see photos of the classroom.

- **Leverage Google Posts:** Share updates, offers, and news to keep your audience engaged and informed.

Importance of Using Keywords in Your Google Business Profile

Using keywords in your Google Business Profile (GBP) is crucial for optimizing your local SEO and improving your business's visibility in search results. Keywords help Google understand the relevance of your business to specific search queries so customers can find you.

Why Keywords Are Important

- **Enhanced Search Visibility:** Keywords help Google match your business with relevant search queries. When users search for products or services you offer, the right keywords can make your profile more likely to appear in their search results.

- **Improved Local SEO:** Incorporating local keywords (e.g., "gun training in Detroit") helps your business appear in local searches, which is crucial for attracting customers in your area.

- **Increased Relevance:** Keywords indicate to Google what your business is about, ensuring that your profile is shown to users interested in your specific products or services.

- **Higher Ranking in Search Results:** Proper keyword usage can improve your ranking in Google's local pack and map results, making your business more visible to potential customers.

- **Targeted Traffic:** Keywords help attract more targeted traffic, meaning visitors who are specifically looking for what you offer, increasing the likelihood of conversions.

Google Business Profile Keywords

For a firearm instructor, using relevant keywords in your Google Business Profile (GBP) can help potential clients find your services more easily. Here's a list of relevant keywords you can incorporate into your GBP to enhance your visibility and attract more targeted traffic:

General Keywords
- Firearm Instructor
- Firearm Training
- Gun Safety Training
- Shooting Lessons
- Firearm Classes
- Gun Training
- Firearms Education
- Firearms Certification
- Gun Handling Training
- Shooting Range Training

Specific Course Keywords
- Concealed Carry Permit Training
- Concealed Carry Classes
- CCW / CPL Training
- Handgun / Pistol / Rifle / Shotgun Training
- Tactical Firearms Training
- Self-Defense Firearm Training
- Advanced Firearm Training

Safety and Legal Keywords
- Gun Safety Courses
- Firearm Safety Certification
- Legal Firearm Ownership Training
- Firearm Laws Education
- Responsible Gun Ownership

Audience-Specific Keywords
- Beginner Firearms Training
- Women's Firearm Training
- Youth Firearm Safety
- Senior Citizen Firearm Training

Location-Specific Keywords
- [City] Firearm Instructor (e.g., "Houston Firearm Instructor")
- [City] Firearms Training (e.g., "Miami Firearms Training")
- [City] Gun Safety Courses (e.g., "Denver Gun Safety Courses")
- Local Firearm Classes
- Nearby Firearms Training

Additional Service Keywords
- Private Firearm Lessons
- Group Firearm Classes
- Corporate Firearm Training
- Firearms Training Workshops
- Range Safety Officer Training

Instruction and Certification Keywords
- USCCA/NRA Certified Instructor
- USCCA/NRA Firearms Training
- USCCA/NRA Courses
- USCCA/NRA Instructor Certification
- USCCA/NRA Safety Courses

Keywords for Specific Needs
- Home Defense Training
- Defensive Shooting Training
- Active Shooter Response Training
- Personal Protection Training
- Marksmanship Training

Example of an Optimized Business Description

"At Elite Firearms Training, our USCCA/NRA certified firearm instructors offer comprehensive gun safety training, concealed carry permit classes, and advanced tactical firearms training in the Miami, Florida area. Whether you're a beginner looking for handgun training or a security professional in need of advanced firearm education, we provide tailored instruction to meet your needs. Join our USCCA/NRA-certified courses for expert guidance and responsible gun ownership education."

Using keywords strategically throughout your Google Business Profile will help improve your visibility, attract the right audience. It's not enough to just set it up, you need to actively engage on it to maintain relevance.

You Need to FEED the Google Machine!

- **Regularly Update Information:** Keep your business hours, address, phone number, and other essential details accurate and up to date. This ensures that customers receive correct information when they find your business on Google.

- **Monitor and Respond to Reviews:** Regularly check for new reviews and respond promptly. Engage with both positive and negative reviews to show responsiveness and customer care, which can positively impact your profile's visibility.

- **Post Regularly:** Use Google Posts to share updates, promotions, events, or news related to your business. Posting regularly not only keeps your profile active but also provides fresh content for potential customers and signals activity to Google.

- **Utilize Photos and Videos:** Continuously update and add high-quality photos and videos that represent your business. Visual content can enhance engagement and provide potential customers with a better understanding of what your business offers.

  Be cautious of posting photos of students unless you have signed a release to do so. Photos of your classroom are highly encouraged – we regularly hear from students who signed in to view the classroom to see what the chairs looked like!

- **Monitor Insights:** Use the Insights section of Google My Business to track how customers are finding your business, what actions they take (like visiting your website or requesting directions), and where they are located. This data can guide your optimization efforts.

- **Add and Update Attributes:** Take advantage of the attributes feature to highlight specific aspects of your business, such as whether you offer handicap-accessible seating, free Wi-Fi, and more. Keeping these attributes updated ensures they accurately reflect your business offerings. It's amazing how listing that you are wheelchair-accessible matters.

You Need to Get Google Reviews

Google Reviews are vital for your business. They shape your online reputation, visibility, and trust. Positive reviews boost your search ranking, making you easier to find. They also offer feedback on your products or services.

Directly Ask Your Customers

- **In-Person Requests:** Politely ask customers for a review after they have completed training. "We hope you enjoyed your experience with us today. Would you mind leaving us a review on Google?"

  You can purchase Google Review Tap Cards by TapFive on Amazon. These smart tap NFC cards allow customers to access your reviews page by simply tapping the card with their mobile phone. They are a great way to collect instant feedback from happy clients.

Printed Materials

- **Receipts and Business Cards**: Include a brief note on receipts or business cards asking for a review, along with a short link or QR code leading to your Google Business Profile.

- **Signage:** Place signs in your classroom encouraging reviews.

Digital Communication

- **Follow-Up Emails**: Send follow-up emails thanking the customer and asking for a review. Include a direct link to your Google Business Profile. For example, "Thank you for your recent visit! We'd love to hear your feedback. Please leave us a review on Google [link]."

- **SMS/Text Messages:** If you have customers' consent to send text messages, you can send a request with a link.

Online and Social Media

- **Website:** Add a section on your website asking for reviews with a direct link to your Google Business Profile.

- **Social Media Posts:** Periodically post on your social media channels, asking satisfied customers to leave a review and providing a link to make it easy.

Providing Easy Access

- **Short Links and QR Codes**: Use tools like Google's URL shortener to create a simple, easy-to-share link. QR codes can also be effective, especially for physical locations. Google provides a shareable link for reviews you can copy and share directly from your Google Business Profile dashboard.

Timing and Personalization

- **Optimal Timing**: Request reviews when the experience is still fresh in the customer's mind, such as immediately after training.

- **Customize Your Message:** Personalize your requests to make customers feel valued. Mention specific details if possible.

SAMPLE SCRIPT: "Hi, Mr./Mrs. Whatever Name - We hope you had a great experience today. If you have a moment, would you please leave us a review on Google? Your feedback helps us improve and helps other customers find us. Thank you!"

You can also encourage your customers to leave honest reviews by offering incentives, such as discounts or coupons. But remember, you cannot buy positive Google reviews. Doing so will get you into trouble with Google and could damage your business's reputation.

Google's review policies are simple but important. They require that reviews be based on personal experiences, relevant to the business, and respectful.

According to Google, "Reviews should represent the genuine experience of the user and should not be written by someone with a conflict of interest." Examples of fake reviews include:

- Reviews written by someone who has never done business with you.

- Reviews are written by someone who is paid to write a positive review.

- Reviews written by someone affiliated with the business, such as an employee, family member, or friend.

"Do something today that your future self will thank you for." - Sean Patrick Flanery"

7 FACEBOOK ADVERTISING

Using Facebook to advertise your business is an effective way to reach a large and targeted audience. I know a lot of instructors that will say "oh, I don't like social media." Hear me out. Like your Google Business Profile - Facebook is GOLD for you as an instructor, whether you like social media or not.

- **Paid Advertising:** Paid advertising on Facebook offers numerous benefits that can significantly enhance your business's online presence and marketing efforts. Understand that while they may agree to run your ad, this might not be the best option for you.

- **FREE Advertising:** Free advertising on Facebook can be highly beneficial for firearms instructors, offering several key advantages over paid ads and without the financial investment required for paid advertising. It's worked for me for years. I'll show you.

Using Facebook as an advertising platform for a firearm instructor can indeed present challenges due to Facebook's stringent policies on firearms.

Facebook's Stance on Firearms - Strict Advertising Policies:

- Facebook has explicit policies that restrict the advertisement of firearms, ammunition, and explosives. This includes not only the sale of these items but also related services and content that promotes their use.

- Ads promoting the sale or use of firearms, ammunition, or explosives are generally prohibited. Up until recently, they allowed brick-and-mortar businesses that were properly licensed by the state and/or federal government to do so, but those days are gone, and I found out the hard way: I posted and got put in time out.

Restricted Content

- Educational content related to firearms, such as training and instructional courses, might also face scrutiny. While Facebook does allow some discussion of firearms for educational or safety purposes, the line between permissible and non-permissible content can be blurry and is often subject to strict interpretation by Facebook's review teams.

- Ads that attempt to circumvent these policies through creative wording or euphemisms often get flagged or rejected. They're on to us. I used to be able to replace the word gun or firearm with an alternate word like heater, blaster, strap, gat, sidearm, roscoe, and the more creative I got, the more creative THEY GOT in banning me. I won't give up.

Challenges for Firearm Instructors

Ad Rejection: Firearm instructors may find that their ads are frequently rejected. Facebook's automated review systems and human moderators can flag and reject ads that mention firearms, even if the ad is for a legal and educational service. The process of appealing these rejections can be time-consuming and may not always result in a successful outcome.

Limited Reach: Due to the restrictive nature of the policies, firearm instructors might struggle to reach their target audience effectively. The inability to promote directly can limit the instructor's ability to attract new clients and grow their business.

Organic reach (non-paid content) may also be limited if the content is deemed to promote firearms. I'll cover shadow banning in a minute. It's a thing.

Content Moderation: Even posts that are not ads but involve firearms can be subject to Facebook's content moderation policies. Educational videos, safety tips, or even discussions about firearm laws can be flagged or removed if they are perceived to violate community standards.

Remember, not everyone is like us. They're scared of guns.

This can result in a significant amount of time spent managing and moderating content to ensure compliance with Facebook's policies.

Workarounds and Alternatives

Compliant Content: Focus on creating content that emphasizes safety, education, and responsible ownership. Avoiding direct sales pitches for firearms and instead promoting broader safety and training content can sometimes bypass restrictions.

Shadow banning is a practice used primarily by social media platforms where a user's content is made less visible or hidden without their knowledge.

The user can still post content and interact with the platform as usual, but their posts and comments are either not shown to others or are given reduced visibility.

This can result in significantly lower engagement on the user's content, as it becomes less accessible to other users.

The goal is often to curb undesirable behavior without alerting the user directly, thus avoiding potential backlash or confrontation.

Some key aspects of shadow banning include:

- **Reduced Visibility:** Your posts and comments are less likely to appear in search results, feeds, or trending lists.

- **Unawareness:** You're typically unaware that they have been shadow-banned, as the platform does not notify you.

- **Temporary or Permanent:** Shadow bans can be temporary, lasting for a specific period, or permanent, depending on the platform's policies and the severity of the violation.

Shadow banning has been a controversial practice in the Facebook world, as it raises concerns about transparency, censorship, and the fair treatment of users.

While Facebook's policies on firearms present significant challenges for advertising, careful navigation of content guidelines, leveraging alternative platforms, and focusing on community-building can help firearm instructors promote their services effectively.

Setting up a PERSONAL Facebook profile is a straightforward process.

Sign Up

- **Visit Facebook:** Go to www.facebook.com

- **Fill in the Sign-Up Form:** On the homepage, you'll see a sign-up form. Enter your first name, last name, mobile number or email address, password, date of birth, etc.

- **Click Sign Up:** After filling in the details, click the "Sign Up" button.

Confirm Your Email or Mobile Number

- **Check Your Email or SMS:** Facebook will send a confirmation code to the email address or mobile number you provided.

- **Enter the Code:** Enter the confirmation code on Facebook to verify your account.

Set Up Your PERSONAL Profile

- **Add a Profile Picture:** Upload a profile picture by clicking on the camera icon on your profile picture placeholder.

- **Add a Cover Photo:** Click on the camera icon on the cover photo placeholder to upload a cover photo. This is the large banner image at the top of your profile.

Complete Your Profile Information

- **About Info:** Click on "About" and fill in details such as your work and education, places you've lived, contact information, and other details.

- **Add Friends:** Search for people you know and send them friend requests. You can find friends by using the search bar at the top of the page or by clicking on "Friends" in the menu.

Create Your First Post

- Share something by writing a status update, uploading a photo or video, or checking in at a location.

Adjust Your PERSONAL Privacy Settings

- **Go to Settings:** Click on the downward-facing arrow at the top right of the Facebook page, select "Settings & Privacy," and then "Settings."

- **Privacy:** In the left-hand menu, click on "Privacy." Here, you can control who can see your posts, who can send you friend requests, and other privacy settings.

- **Timeline & Tagging:** Adjust who can post on your timeline and who can tag you in posts.

- **Security and Login:** Enhance the security of your account by setting up two-factor authentication and monitoring where you're logged in.

THIS IS THE MOST IMPORTANT PART - JOIN GROUPS

- **Join Groups:** This is where the magic happens!! You will want to join as many LOCAL groups as possible for your general area.

Search for community groups for your city, and neighboring towns, buy and sell groups, and small business and networking groups.

You do this by going to your Facebook page and clicking on the Groups icon on the far left. It will open the Groups page where it will offer group suggestions based on your location.

You'll be joining these groups from your **PERSONAL** profile because they are more apt to allow you to join as a person, rather than as a business.

There are public and private groups - it makes no difference; some are just easier to get in than others.

Some groups will allow you in immediately, others ask a series of questions before you are considered a member with posting privileges, and it may take a week or so before you are allowed to post.

Use the Search Groups area to list additional city names for more group options. Think creatively and join, join, join!

Setting Up a BUSINESS Facebook Page

Whether you should set up a business Facebook page separate from your personal Facebook account depends on your specific needs and privacy concerns. Here are some considerations to help you decide:

Pros of Using a Personal Account to Set Up a Business Page

- **Ease of Access:** It's easier to manage since you don't need to switch accounts.

- **Integration:** You can quickly share posts from your business page to your personal timeline to increase reach.

- **Permissions:** You can easily assign roles to other people to help manage the page.

- **Analytics and Ads:** All your analytics and ad management tools are conveniently accessible from one account.

- **Joining Groups:** It's been my experience that you'll find getting accepted into community Groups easier if you are trying to join them as a person rather than as a business.

Cons of Using a Personal Account to Set Up a Business Page

- **Privacy Concerns:** There is potential for overlap between personal and business activities, which might affect your privacy.

- **Professionalism:** Having a separate business account can make it appear more professional to clients and customers.

- **Management Complexity:** If multiple people need to manage the business page, using a personal account can complicate role assignments and permissions.

Pros of Setting Up a Separate Business Facebook Account

- **Privacy:** Keep your personal and business activities separate.

- **Professional Image:** May project a more professional image to customers and clients.

- **Security:** Limits the risk of accessing or confusing personal information with business information.

Cons of Setting Up a Separate Business Facebook Account

- **Management:** Requires switching between accounts, which can be inconvenient.

- **Duplicate Effort:** You might need to maintain separate friends/contacts lists if you want to promote your business through both accounts.

Recommendations

- Use Your Personal Account but Adjust Privacy Settings.

- Create the business page from your personal account, but use Facebook's privacy settings to manage the personal information that is visible to your business page followers.

- Only your name and public information will be linked to the business page; your personal posts and profile details remain private unless you choose to share them.

Again, we have found it easier to join Groups using a personal Facebook page vs. a business page. Facebook Groups are a direct line to customers, allowing you to really build a community around your brand, making you more valuable.

Our goal with joining the groups is to list our class information in the Events areas of the groups, post our ads if allowed, and participate as a subject matter expert in our community.

Setting up a Business Facebook from Your Personal Facebook Account

Setting up a Facebook page for your business from your personal account is a straightforward process. Here's a step-by-step guide to help you get started:

Log In to Your Personal Facebook Account - Create a Page

- Navigate to the Facebook homepage.

- On the left sidebar, find and click on "Pages."

- Click on the "Create New Page" button.

Enter Page Information

- **Page Name:** Enter the name of your business.

- **Category:** Select the most relevant option from the dropdown menu. You can add up to three categories. Education, School, and Sports & Fitness Instruction are good choices.

- **Description:** Provide a brief description of up to 255 characters.

Customize Your Page

- **Profile Picture:** Upload a profile picture. This is usually your business logo. The recommended size is 170x170 pixels.

- **Cover Photo:** Upload a cover photo that represents your business. The recommended size is 820x312 pixels.

Add Additional Information

- **Username:** Create a username for your page. This makes it easier for people to find your page (e.g., @YourBusinessName).

- **Contact Information:** Add your business phone number, email, and website.

- **Location:** If you have a physical location, add the address.

- **Hours:** List business hours - make them attractive to customers.

Publish Your Page

- Review all the information you've entered.

- Once you are satisfied with everything, click the "Publish Page" button.

Add Content to Your Page

- **Posts:** Start posting content related to your business and post regularly. We post memes regularly - be careful, though - Facebook is watching and looking for things they deem "harmful." I'll share more on this later.

- **Call to Action:** Add a call-to-action button like "Contact Us," "Shop Now," or "Learn More" to encourage engagement.

- **Add Classes to Events:** Go to the events area and populate it with all of your upcoming class information.

By populating your Upcoming Events section, potential clients who visit your Facebook page can see all of the classes you have coming up.

Promote Your Page!

- **Share your page:** Share your new business page on your personal timeline. Ask all your Facebook friends and family to share your page.

  Go to your Business page, and you will see three dots . . . on the right side of the page. **Click them** and choose *INVITE FRIENDS*. You can then bulk invite anyone you have friended on your Facebook page.

  Then, ask the people who have liked your page to have the friends and family they have on their Facebook page do the same thing.

  You will easily gain hundreds of Facebook followers in a very short period following this method.

FREE Facebook Advertising

Create and Optimize Your Facebook Business Page

Complete Your Profile

- Ensure all business details are filled out completely, including your business name, address, phone number, website, and business hours.

- Use a professional profile picture (your logo) and a cover photo.

About Section

Write a compelling "About" section that clearly describes all the training services you offer. Remember to use as many keywords as possible in a conversational manner.

Post Regularly and Consistently - Share Engaging Content

- Post a variety of content types, including images, videos, blog posts, and updates about your business.

- Share behind-the-scenes looks, customer testimonials, product updates, and industry news.

- **Run contests!** The Detroit Lions were **ON FIRE** this past season. Every game day we ran a "give us the correct final score and winning team name by halftime" game - offering a free class to the winner. TONS of activity on the page. We ran this contest **ALL SEASON**, got thousands of views, shares and likes and subsequently new followers, and only ever had **ONE** winner!

Use High-Quality Visuals

Ensure your images and videos are high-quality and relevant to your audience. Avoid political-leaning commentary.

Post at Optimal Times

Experiment with posting at different times to determine when your audience is most active. I find my followers most active mid-day (Noon) and evening (after 7:00 pm)

Viral Potential

- **Shares and Recommendations:** Your followers can share quality content, increasing your reach exponentially without additional cost. We post a variety of funny, informative, advertising, and news articles regarding safety and self-defense. Every time someone shares something they've seen on your page – everyone on their page will see your business information. THIS IS HUGE!

- **User-Generated Content:** Encouraging customers to share their experiences and tag your business can create organic buzz and social proof. Have students take photos at the class and SHARE!

- **Narrative Sharing:** Share your business story, mission, and values through regular posts to connect with your audience on a personal level. We have an entire series of "Did You Know" posts that drop little tidbits of information to generate interest in learning more.

Visual Branding

Consistent posting of branded images, videos, and graphics helps reinforce your brand identity. We have an entire series of ads for our Michigan Concealed Carry class. Every single ad varies in content and look except for the bright yellow business card they see displayed in every ad. This breeds familiarity.

Improved SEO and Online Presence

- **Search Engine Visibility:** Regular activity on your Facebook page can improve your business's visibility in search engine results, driving more traffic to your website.

- **Cross-Platform Integration:** Sharing your Facebook content on other platforms (like your website, blog, or other social media accounts) can enhance your overall online presence.

Valuable Insights and Analytics

- **Facebook Page Insights:** Even without paid ads, Facebook provides valuable analytics on your page's performance, audience demographics, and post engagement, helping you refine your content strategy. In your professional dashboard, you can see how your page activity stacks up - post reach, post engagement, new page likes, and more.

Content Experimentation

- **Testing and Learning:** You can experiment with different types of content (videos, images, text posts) to see what resonates best with your audience without the pressure of ad spend.

Utilizing FREE Facebook Features

- **Facebook Groups:** Joining and actively participating in Facebook groups in your community can help you connect with potential customers and establish your expertise.

- **Facebook Events:** Creating and promoting events (webinars, workshops, in-person classes) can help you engage with your audience in real-time and drive participation.

Customer Service and Feedback

- **Direct Interaction:** Use your Facebook page to answer customer inquiries, handle complaints, and gather feedback, improving customer satisfaction and loyalty.

- **Review and Ratings:** Encourage satisfied customers to leave positive reviews on your page, enhancing your business's reputation. While having reviews on Facebook doesn't count toward your Google Business Profile reviews and rankings, it's still an effective platform for customer reviews.

RECAP

- **Post Regularly:** Maintain a consistent posting schedule to keep your audience engaged.

- **Engage with Followers:** Respond to comments and messages.

- **Create Quality Content:** Focus on high-quality, valuable content.

- **Encourage User-Generated Content:** Motivate customers to share their experiences with you.

Use eye-catching, descriptive ads...

Have a consistent "theme" with the ads you post across Facebook. There is a marketing principle that customers need to see your brand at least seven times before they commit to a purchase decision. Make sure they know it's YOU.

Share firearm-related memes on your Facebook page to encourage customer activity.

Visit the Facebook page for Detroit Arms.

You'll see that we integrate a variety of ads, local news articles, and memes relating to being a gun owner. I can't share the photos here due to copyright laws (I don't need any lawsuits). Just know that every time these memes are shared, so is our business name & information.

Anything to generate interest, get them talking or laughing and sharing.

HOWEVER - You can find yourself in "trouble" with Facebook if they deem your meme "inappropriate", if they do, they will put you in a "time out" where you will not be able to post on your page. It doesn't matter that you got it off Facebook to begin with. Go figure.

Depending on the current number of "infractions" you have, it could be as short as 24 hours and forever—their choice. You can try and fight it. I do and win "most" of the time.

Every reaction also allows you to invite that individual to like your page, which quickly adds new followers to your brand.

Every share is to a potential client.

- **Respond to Comments and Messages:** Engage with your followers by responding to their comments and messages promptly and professionally. Address any questions or concerns they may have. The fact that you have people sharing your content on their own page may mean you pick up an anti-gun troll here and there. Play nice.

- **Encourage Interaction:** Ask questions and encourage followers to share their opinions and experiences.

Customer Engagement

The idea is to keep your page active to gain new visitors. To encourage customer engagement and activity on your Facebook page, you might consider:

Product/Service Highlights

- **New Arrivals/Launches:** Showcase new classes or services to generate excitement.

- **Best Sellers:** Highlight popular classes to attract interest from potential customers.

- **Behind-the-scenes:** Share photos or videos showing excerpts from your class - before doing so, make sure your students have permission to post them publicly.

Customer Interaction

- **Testimonials/Reviews:** Post positive reviews or testimonials from satisfied customers – even if it means cut and paste from your Google Business Profile reviews.

- **Customer Spotlights:** Feature stories or photos of happy customers.

- **Q&A Sessions:** Host Facebook live events or scheduled Q&A sessions to answer customer queries.

Promotions and Offers

- **Exclusive Discounts:** Offer special Facebook-only discounts or deals.

- **Giveaways and Contests:** Run contests or giveaways to engage followers and increase visibility. We often run sports contests - ex. "Tell us the winning team and exact final score by halftime and you'll win a FREE class!" We ran this promo all football season last year and only had ONE winner! Pick any sport – keeps you busy all year!

- **Flash Sales:** Announce limited-time offers to create urgency.

Educational Content

- **How-To Guides:** Share tutorials or how-to videos related to firearm training. Show photos of proper grip, stance, and differences between ammunition. How to choose a firearm, a holster, etc.

- **Tips and Tricks:** Provide useful tips that can help your customers. We regularly post little tidbits about things like rules for Open Carry (many people don't understand the intricacies of the law, so we point them out), Did You Know for alerting to things that may cause one to break the law (because they didn't KNOW the law), etc.

Community Engagement

- **Local Events:** Promote local events or your participation in community activities.

- **Partnerships:** Highlight collaborations with other local businesses or organizations. We partner with a local range and interchange, sharing each other's posts.

- **Charity Work:** Showcase your involvement in charitable activities or donations. Detroit Arms donates a lot of gift certificates to local fundraiser events, so we share the information on the events to encourage attendance and the chance to win a class.

Interactive Content

- **Polls and Surveys:** Conduct polls or surveys to gather feedback.

- **Quizzes:** Create fun and relevant quizzes that your followers can participate in.

- **Challenges:** Initiate challenges that encourage followers to participate and share their experiences. Show us your last target – and discuss!

User-Generated Content

- **Customer Photos/Videos:** Encourage customers to share photos or videos using your products and repost them.

- **Testimonials and Reviews:** Ask customers to leave reviews and share them on your page.

Seasonal Content

- **Holiday Posts:** Create posts related to holidays and seasonal events. It doesn't even have to be a "real" holiday! Celebrate 2/23 as .223 Day or 4/10 as .410 Day.

Behind-the-Scenes Content

- **Day in the Life:** Show what a typical day looks like at your business.

- **Team Introductions:** Introduce yourself and your team members.

Inspirational and Motivational Posts

- **Quotes:** Share inspiring or motivational quotes related to firearm ownership.

- **Success Stories:** Highlight success stories, either from you personally or your customers.

Industry News and Updates

- **Trends:** Share the latest trends to position yourself as a knowledgeable leader. People always want to know what the newest holster innovation is, the newest gun on the market, etc.

- **News Articles:** Post relevant news articles that might interest your audience.

- **Product Recall Alerts:** Let customers know about guns and gun related items that may have a current recall issued.

- **Law Changes:** Have there been recent updates to firearm laws in your area? Make sure you post them for your clients to see.

Posting in Facebook Groups

Posting in Groups on Facebook is a great way to reach your local market without spending any financial resources to do so. Your only investment is your time.

You can utilize groups for two specific purposes - actually posting your class and training offerings in the general conversation of the group (if allowed) and adding your class dates and times to the Events section of a group.

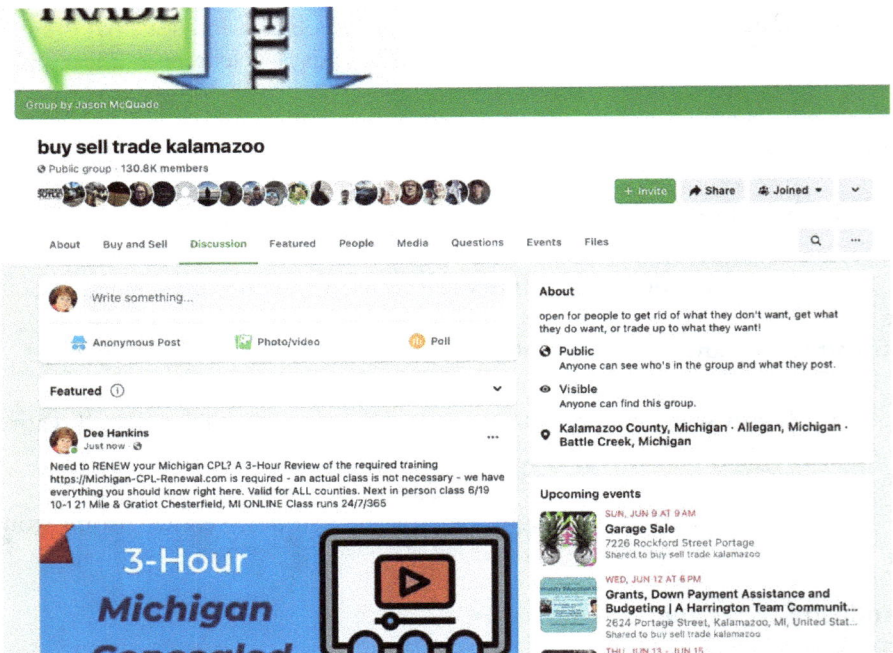

This group, for example, is 170 miles from us. I don't anticipate anyone from this group ever traveling to Detroit Arms for training.

HOWEVER, I do host a video-on-demand course that is applicable to Michigan residents in that area. You'll notice there are over 130,000 people in this group - not too shabby. There are dozens of groups for just that area of Michigan alone.

Macomb County Sales
Public group · 38.7K members

About | Buy and Sell | **Discussion** | People | Media | Events | Files

Write something...

Reel | Photo/video | Poll

Featured

Dee Hankins
Just now

Need to RENEW your Michigan CPL? A 3-Hour Review of the required training https://Michigan-CPL-Renewal.com is required - an actual class is not necessary - we have everything you should know right here. Valid for ALL counties. Next in person class 6/19 10-1 21 Mile & Gratiot Chesterfield, MI ONLINE Class runs 24/7/365

3-Hour Michigan Concealed Pistol License

About

Post anything for sale or trade. Only rule is if it is a trade then you must have a trade value or it will be deleted. Any questions feel free t... See more

Public
Anyone can see who's in the group and what they post.

Visible
Anyone can find this group.

Roseville, Michigan

Upcoming events

HAPPENING NOW
Big Daddys Garage Sale
11848 Farnum Ave, Warren, MI 48093-4622, Unit . Shared to Buy, Sell or Trade in Macomb Township, MI (No Childrens Items)

TOMORROW AT 8 AM
CPL Certification class
3285 Carrigan Road Fort Gratiot, MI 48059
Professional networking · Shared to Blue Water Area Sales

WED, JUN 19 AT 10 AM
Michigan Concealed Carry CCW/CPL Class
Detroit Arms The Michigan CPL Pros
for Macomb County Sales

This is a group right in our backyard. We are in Macomb County, Michigan. This Group allows for not only posting in the Discussion section but also placing our class information in the Events section. There are over 38,000 members in this group.

Always make sure that you understand the guidelines for posting in a Group before you blast your information on it. You'll find guidelines for posting in a Group in the About section.

Many groups require that you be a member for a pre-determined number of days (typically a week) before you are allowed to post. Other Groups require an Administrator to approve your posts before they appear. Other Groups only allow businesses to post on a specific day of the week. Some only allow you to post in the Upcoming Events section and not in the general conversation section.

A word of caution - Facebook will think you are "spamming" if you post into too many Groups in quick succession. Only post to a couple dozen at any given time. Put some time in between your posting sessions, otherwise you will find yourself in "time out". Been there. Done that.

Find & Join Local Buy/Sell/Community/Small Business Groups

Join Facebook groups where your target audience is likely to be active. You'll find lots of options by searching using your city and county name. Choose surrounding communities as well. Facebook will also begin suggesting groups to you as you join.

Participate Actively

- Engage in discussions, answer questions, and share valuable insights without directly selling your products.

- Position yourself as a helpful and knowledgeable member of the community.

- Add Your Classes to the Event Sections. Most local community groups and buy/sell groups have an Events tab.

Free advertising opportunities on Facebook can be highly beneficial for firearm instructors, offering several key advantages without the financial investment required for paid advertising.

Cost-Effective Marketing

- **No Financial Investment:** Free advertising methods, such as organic posts, cost nothing but your time and effort, making it an ideal option for businesses with limited budgets.

- **Building Organic Reach and Engagement:** Organic posts often result in more genuine interactions and engagement, as users who follow your page are generally more interested in your content.

- **Community Building:** Regularly posting and interacting with your audience helps build a loyal community around your brand.

- **Enhanced Credibility and Trust:** Organic content can be perceived as more authentic and trustworthy by users, as it's not explicitly labeled as an advertisement.

- **Customer Relationships:** Engaging directly with customers through comments and messages fosters stronger relationships and trust.

PAID Facebook Advertising

While organic growth is important for building a loyal and engaged audience over time, paid Facebook advertising offers immediate and scalable benefits that can significantly enhance reach, engagement, and conversion rates.

Facebook ads offer significant advantages and some drawbacks for firearm instructors.

On the positive side, Facebook ads provide immediate reach and visibility, allowing you to target specific demographics, interests, and behaviors, ensuring their ads reach the most relevant audiences. The platform's advanced targeting options and detailed analytics enable precise control and optimization of ad campaigns, maximizing return on investment.

Additionally, Facebook ads can complement organic efforts, amplifying overall brand presence. However, the cons include the risk of wasting the budget if ads are not properly targeted or managed.

EVERY DAY, I see Facebook ads for firearms instructors that are hundreds, if not THOUSANDS of miles outside my market in my own personal Facebook feed.

Why?

They missed a crucial setting on the dashboard and didn't narrow the delivery area for the ad.

Furthermore, poorly designed ads can lead to low engagement and a negative perception of the brand.

The competitive nature of the platform can also drive up costs, making it challenging for small businesses with limited budgets.

Finally, navigating Facebook's ad policies and ensuring compliance can be complex and time-consuming.

Therefore, while Facebook ads offer powerful tools for growth, we must approach them strategically to avoid potential pitfalls.

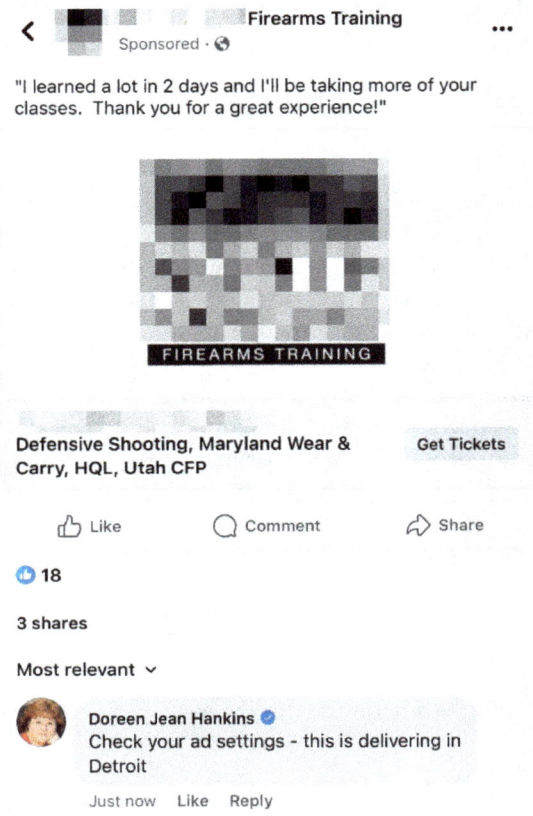

This ad, for example, is for a firearm training company 568 miles from where the ad was delivering. The names have been blurred to protect the innocent.

Utilizing PAID Facebook Advertising

To utilize paid advertising on Facebook, aka Sponsored Posts, you must follow several essential steps to set up and manage your campaigns effectively:

Set Up Your Facebook Business Page

- Go to Facebook and click on the "Create" button, then select "Page."

- Choose "Business or Brand" and follow the prompts to enter your business details and set up your page.

Complete Your Business Page

- Add a profile picture (your logo) and a cover photo that represents your brand.

- Fill in all the necessary information, such as your business name, address, phone number, website, and business hours.

- Write a compelling "About" section to describe your business and what you offer.

Define Your Advertising Goals

Determine what you want to achieve with your Facebook ads.

- **Brand Awareness:** Increase awareness of your business.
- **Website Traffic:** Drive visitors to your website or landing page.
- **Engagement:** Boost likes, comments, shares, etc.
- **Event Promotion:** Drive students to sign up for an event or class.
- **Lead Generation:** Collect contact information.
- **Conversions:** Drive sales or specific actions on your website.

Access Facebook Ads Manager

- Access Ads Manager through your business page or directly by visiting business.facebook.com.

- If you don't already have an account, you'll need to set one up.

Create Your Ad Campaign

- Click the "Create" button and select the objective that aligns with your advertising goals.

Set Up Your Ad Account

- Enter your account details, including your country, currency, and time zone.

Define Your Target Audience

- Use Facebook's targeting options to define your audience based on demographics (age, gender, location), interests, behaviors, and more.

- You can create a custom audience using customer lists, website traffic, or app activity.

Set Your Budget and Schedule

- Choose between a daily budget or a lifetime budget.

- Set the start and end dates for your ad campaign, or let it run continuously.

Choose Your Ad Placement

- Select where you want your ads to appear (e.g., Facebook News Feed, Instagram, Audience Network, Messenger).

- You can use automatic placements or manually select your placements.

Create Your Ad

- **Choose Your Ad Format:** Facebook offers various ad formats, including image ads, video ads, carousel ads, slideshow ads, and collection ads. Choose the format that best suits your objective.

- **Add Media and Text:** Upload high-quality images or videos that are relevant to your ad. Write compelling ad copy that grabs attention and communicates your message. Include a strong call-to-action (CTA) to guide users on what to do next.

Preview Your Ad

- Review how your ad will look on different devices and placements to ensure it is visually appealing and correctly formatted.

Launch Your Campaign

- Review and Submit:

- Double-check all your ad settings, including your target audience, budget, and ad creatives.

- Click the "Confirm" button to submit your ad for review.

Monitor and Optimize

- Once your ad is live, monitor its performance through Facebook Ads Manager.

- Track key metrics such as reach, engagement, clicks, and conversions.

- Use insights to optimize your ads, adjusting targeting, budget, and creatives.

Analyze Results and Refine Your Strategy

- **Analyze Performance Data:** Review the performance of your ad campaigns using Facebook's reporting tools.

- Identify which ads are performing well and which ones need improvement.

Refine Your Strategy

- Use the data to make informed decisions about your future campaigns.

- Test different ad formats, targeting options, and ad creatives to find what works best for your audience.

Retargeting

- Use Facebook's retargeting capabilities to reach people who have already interacted with your business, such as visiting your website or engaging with your posts.

By following these steps and continuously refining your approach based on performance data, you can effectively use Facebook to advertise your business and achieve your marketing goals.

A WORD OF CAUTION

I said it earlier, and I'll repeat it because it bears repeating - **EVERY DAY,** I see Facebook ads in my feed for firearms instructors **WAY** outside of their market.

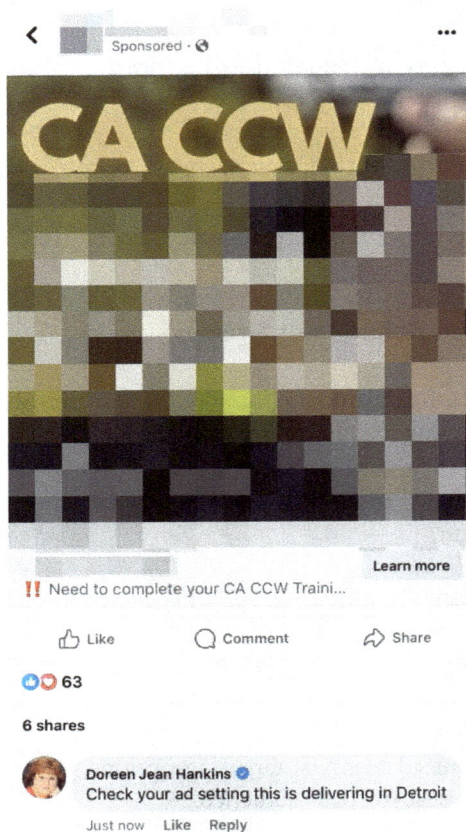

California is 2,400 miles from Detroit. This means their ad budget is being blown on wasted ads in markets that will likely never buy from them.

Paid advertising on Facebook offers numerous benefits that can significantly enhance your business's online presence and marketing efforts.

Precise Targeting

- **Demographic Targeting**: Target audiences based on age, gender, location, and other demographic factors.

- **Interest and Behavior Targeting:** Reach users based on their interests, behaviors, and activities on Facebook.

- **Custom Audiences:** Upload customer lists to target existing customers or website visitors.

- **Lookalike Audiences:** Target new potential customers who have characteristics similar to those of your existing audience.

Extended Reach and Visibility

- **Increased Reach:** Paid ads can reach a larger and more diverse audience beyond your existing followers.

- **Visibility Across Platforms:** Ads can appear not only on Facebook but also on Instagram, Messenger, and the Audience Network, maximizing exposure.

Measurable Results

- Detailed Analytics: Access comprehensive insights and analytics to track the performance of your ads, including reach, engagement, click-through rates, and conversions.

- Real-Time Reporting: Monitor your ad performance in real-time and make decisions to optimize your ad.

Cost-Effective and Flexible Budgeting

- Control Over Budget: Set daily or lifetime budgets.

- Adjustable Spending: Adjust your spending at any time based on performance and business needs.
- Cost-Per-Click (CPC) and Cost-Per-Impression (CPM) Options

Enhanced Engagement

- **Interactive Ad Formats:** A variety of ad formats such as carousel, video, and collection ads engage your audience.

- **Promote Specific Actions:** Drive specific actions such as website visits, lead generation, and event attendance with tailored ads.

A/B Testing and Optimization

- **Split Testing:** Test different ad creatives, headlines, audiences, and placements to determine what works best in attracting potential clients.

- **Continuous Optimization:** Use the data from A/B tests to refine and improve your ad campaigns continuously.

Improved Brand Awareness

- **Broader Audience:** Increase brand recognition by consistently exposing your business to a broad and relevant audience.

- **Consistent Messaging:** Reinforce your brand message through consistent and strategic ad placements.

Retargeting Capabilities

- **Remarketing:** Show ads to users who have previously interacted with your website, app, or Facebook content, encouraging them to return and complete desired actions.

- **Dynamic Ads:** Automatically show personalized ads featuring products or services that users have shown interest in.

Access to Professional Tools

- **Facebook Pixel:** Implement the Facebook Pixel on your website to track conversions, optimize ads, and build targeted audiences based on site traffic.

  Custom Conversions: Define and track specific customer actions that matter most to your business.

Scalability

- Small to Large Scale: Start with a small budget and scale up as you see positive results, making it accessible for businesses of all sizes.

You can also start and stop ads at any time, without penalty, which is helpful if you find a particular ad is not delivering the desired results or if you have simply just decided to try other avenues.

Successfully leveraging paid advertising on Facebook requires a systematic approach, from setting up your Business Page and Ads Account to defining clear objectives, creating compelling ads, and continuously monitoring performance.

Proper execution and adherence to Facebook's policies are key to achieving desired results and maximizing your advertising investment.
If you are wondering how WE do it... Detroit Arms does not utilize Facebook for sponsored ads. We have found greater success with the organic methods we have described earlier.

ZERO Paid Advertising?

Correct. Zero.

I know that's totally underwhelming, but it came to be this way for good reason.
Let me be clear. Zero spend in paid ads has not always been the case.

Back when Facebook was in its infancy, and up until about five years ago, we spent hundreds of dollars a month on promoted ads. It is a way different machine today than it was years ago. Censorship has reared its ugly head. Guns are not a favored topic, and the restrictions on what you can and can't post about have gotten stricter over the years. Thanks to AI scanning, now it's even worse.

The same goes for Google, Nextdoor, Yelp, the local newspaper(s), direct mail, family diner coffee mugs and placemats, Valpak, radio ads, the list goes on and on. As time went on, we discovered our paid efforts for advertising were just not returning the results you'd expect based on the dollar amount spent.

While there is a trade-off between paid advertising and organic reach advertising (in that you must manually input some of the information yourself), it has its benefits.

"Opportunities don't happen. You create them." - Chris Grosser.

8 UTILIZING OTHER SOCIAL MEDIA PLATFORMS

For firearm instructors, leveraging a variety of social media platforms can be a powerful way to reach potential customers, engage with the community, and build brand awareness.

Each social media platform attracts different user demographics. For instance, Instagram and TikTok have a younger user base, while LinkedIn caters to professionals and businesses.

By diversifying platforms, you can reach various segments of your market. Relying on a single platform is risky due to potential algorithm changes or policy shifts. Diversifying reduces the risk of losing reach or engagement due to changes on one platform.

Having a presence on multiple social media platforms enhances reach, brand recognition, and credibility.

Utilizing Other Social Media Platforms - Some Popular Choices

Instagram

- **Visual Focus:** Ideal for visual content like photos and short videos. Use it to showcase classes, share tips, and engage with a younger audience.

- **Engagement:** High engagement rates through posts, stories, reels.

- **Demographics:** Popular among younger audiences, particularly millennials and Gen Z.

- **Advertising:** You can post free, or you can run ads from your Instagram professional account and use Meta tools to create ads that appear on both Instagram and Facebook.

Twitter/X

- **Real-Time Updates:** Useful for sharing updates, engaging in conversations, and following industry trends. Ideal for concise communication.

- **Hashtags:** Effective use of hashtags can increase visibility and engagement.

- **Character Limit:** The 280-character limit encourages concise and impactful messaging.

- **Demographics:** Broad user base, strong presence of professionals and tech-savvy users.

- **Advertising:** Offers a wide variety of free and paid options.

TikTok

- **Short-Form Video Content:** Great for short, engaging, and creative videos. Suitable for quick tips, demonstrations, and reaching a younger audience.

- **Wide Reach:** Potential for videos to go viral, reaching a global audience.

- **Demographics:** Highly popular among Gen Z but gaining traction with older demographics as well.

- **Advertising:** Offers various advertising options, including in-feed ads, branded hashtags, and branded effects.

Nextdoor

- **Local Focus:** Best for businesses targeting local communities. Users are primarily neighbors and residents in your geographical area.

- **Community Engagement:** Facilitates word-of-mouth recommendations and direct engagement with local customers.

- **Demographics:** Often used by homeowners and individuals interested in finding training and services in their local area, including older demographics.

- **Advertising:** Offers the ability to post free and has paid ad options.

LinkedIn

- **Professional Network:** THE platform for business - essential for B2B business engagement, offering professional services, and branding.

- **Content Types:** Articles, professional updates, company news.

- **Demographics:** Professionals, business owners.

- **Advertising:** Offers the ability to post free and paid ad options.

YouTube

- **Long-Form Video Content:** Perfect for tutorials, product reviews, behind-the-scenes content, and vlogs.

- **SEO Benefits:** Videos can rank on both YouTube and Google, driving traffic and visibility.

- **Monetization:** Opportunities through ads, memberships, and super chats.

- **Demographics:** Broad audience across various age groups.

- **Advertising:** Offers the ability to post free and has paid ad options.

How Do I Choose?

Evaluate Your Preferred Content-Type and Frequency

- **Visual Content** (Photos/Videos): Instagram, YouTube, TikTok

- **Written Content** (Articles/Updates): Facebook, LinkedIn, Twitter

- **Live Streaming:** Instagram, Facebook, YouTube

Consider Platform Growth and Trends

- Stay updated with trends and changes in platform algorithms.

- Evaluate emerging platforms that might align with your goals.

Assess Your Resources

- **Time:** How much time can you dedicate to content creation and engagement?

- **Skills:** Are you comfortable with video editing, photography, writing, etc.?

- **Budget:** Do you have a budget for ads, professional content creation, or platform-specific tools?

Experiment and Analyze

- Start with a couple of platforms that seem most promising.

- Track your performance using analytics tools provided by the platforms.

- Adjust your strategy based on what works best in terms of engagement and reach.

Community and Compliance

- Be aware of each platform's policies on firearm-related content.

"The secret of business is to know something that nobody else knows."
- Aristotle Onassis

9 ADDITIONAL LOW-COST MARKETING STRATEGIES

Launching a firearm instruction business requires effective marketing strategies that don't break the bank.

Low-cost and no-cost advertising is crucial, especially those instructors just starting out, due to limited financial resources and the need to establish a presence in a competitive market.

By leveraging cost-effective advertising methods, you can maximize your visibility and reach potential customers without the burden of high expenses.

Heck, even seasoned veterans of the industry need to keep advertising costs under control. In fact, much of what I'm about to share with you are things that Detroit Arms does on a regular basis to this very day!!

Email Marketing

- Send out a regular newsletter with updates, tips, and special offers.

Referral Programs

- Offer discounts or free sessions to clients who refer new customers to you. Satisfied clients can be your best marketers.

- Allow Alumni to attend the class again FREE if they bring you a paying client. This works especially well for concealed carry classes - we allow the alumni to attend the classroom portion but not typically the range portion as there are costs involved in doing so.

- Host free introductory classes or safety seminars. This can attract new clients and give them a taste of what you offer. Consider conducting free online webinars on specific topics related to firearm training and safety.

- Work with local schools, scout groups, or other organizations to provide educational workshops such as firearm safety awareness. This can position you as a responsible and knowledgeable instructor in the community.

Printed Materials

- Distribute flyers and brochures in local gun shops, community centers, and sporting goods stores. At Detroit Arms we hang signs listing class dates and pull tabs. We also leave behind brochures for the stores.

DETROIT ARMS, LLC **$125.00** **DETROIT ARMS, LLC**

Michigan Concealed Carry
CCW/CPL PERMIT CLASS

ALL IN-PERSON TRAINING – USCCA CERTIFIED INSTRUCTORS – 16+ YEARS IN THE INDUSTRY

1-Day ALL IN PERSON Class

SCAN

Wednesday, June 19, 2024
10:00 am - 7:00 pm

Sunday, June 23, 2024
10:00 am - 7:00 pm

Saturday, June 29, 2024
10:00 am - 7:00 pm

Sunday, July 14, 2024
10:00 am - 7:00 pm

Saturday, July 27, 2024
10:00 am - 7:00 pm

Saturday, August 17, 2024
10:00 am - 7:00 pm

Sunday, August 25, 2024
10:00 am - 7:00 pm

SCAN

Detroit Arms 25986 S. Knollwood Chesterfield, MI 48051
Off Gratiot, north of 21 Mile in the Apple Grove Shopping Plaza

Valid for ALL Michigan Counties & 39 States

Includes hot lunch, FREE firearm rental, indoor range time & more!

Register: www.DetroitArms.com Call: 586-598-5300

Detroit Arms – CCW/CPL Classes www.DetroitArms.com 586-598-5300 1-DAY Michigan Concealed Carry Classes

Detroit Arms – CCW/CPL Classes www.DetroitArms.com 586-598-5300 1-DAY Michigan Concealed Carry Classes

Detroit Arms – CCW/CPL Classes www.DetroitArms.com 586-598-5300 1-DAY Michigan Concealed Carry Classes

Detroit Arms – CCW/CPL Classes www.DetroitArms.com 586-598-5300 1-DAY Michigan Concealed Carry Classes

Detroit Arms – CCW/CPL Classes www.DetroitArms.com 586-598-5300 1-DAY Michigan Concealed Carry Classes

Detroit Arms – CCW/CPL Classes www.DetroitArms.com 586-598-5300 1-DAY Michigan Concealed Carry Classes

Detroit Arms – CCW/CPL Classes www.DetroitArms.com 586-598-5300 1-DAY Michigan Concealed Carry Classes

Detroit Arms – CCW/CPL Classes www.DetroitArms.com 586-598-5300 1-DAY Michigan Concealed Carry Classes

- **Business Cards!** Always have business cards on hand. Leave them behind at local businesses that will allow you to do so. We have several local restaurants and stores that allow us to leave stacks of cards by the cash register.

Donating gift certificates to local fundraisers is a strategic way for you to generate increased visibility and customer engagement within your community. By contributing gift certificates to local events and fundraisers, it not only demonstrates your commitment to supporting the community, but also effectively promotes your business to a wider audience.

Fundraisers typically attract a diverse group of attendees, many of whom may not be familiar with you.

Donating to fundraisers helps build a positive brand image and fosters goodwill.

Community members often remember and appreciate businesses that actively participate in local causes, which can enhance the business's reputation and lead to word-of-mouth referrals.

This type of grassroots marketing is invaluable for small businesses as it leverages the power of community connections and trust. Additionally, fundraisers often recognize their sponsors in promotional materials, social media, and during the event itself, providing the business with additional exposure.

At Detroit Arms, we donate gift certificates regularly.

The key is to donate ONE.

If you donate two, you give up the opportunity for a person to win one and then bring a paying friend.

"If opportunity doesn't knock, build a door."
- Milton Berle

10 GROWING YOUR BUSINESS

Growing your business as a firearm trainer is a journey that demands both patience and persistence. "Build it, and they will come" only works in the movies. It's important to remember that success doesn't happen overnight; it's the result of consistent effort and dedication.

Every class you teach, every client you engage with, and every skill you impart contributes to the reputation and growth of your firearm training business. What may seem like nothing to you can help train someone to save their life.

Embrace each challenge as an opportunity to refine your methods and enhance your expertise. The effort you put into building a solid foundation today will pay off in the long run, attracting more clients through word-of-mouth and positive reviews.

Persistence is equally crucial. There will be days when progress seems slow, or obstacles appear insurmountable. Trust us. Been there. Done that. During these times, staying focused on your goals and maintaining a positive attitude can make all the difference.

Look back on what's worked in the past and continue to refine your marketing strategies, continuously improve your teaching techniques, diligently spread your message and always seek feedback from your clients to understand their needs so you can better serve them as well as your future clients.

Remember, every small step forward is progress.

Success is not owned; it is rented - and that rent is due every day. Success comes down to choosing the hard right over the easy wrong. Consistently. - Rory Vaden

By staying patient and persistent, you not only build a successful business but also become a trusted and respected figure in your community.

Your dedication will inspire confidence in your clients, ultimately leading to sustained growth and success.

Given the shift towards constitutional carry in many states, a number of firearm trainers have struggled to find enough clients to keep them consistently busy.

After all, if one isn't required to take state mandated training in order to receive a license carry a firearm in my state, why train at all?

There are SO MANY valid reasons why, and it's our job to educate the public.

Many people don't realize that while their state allows residents to carry a concealed firearm without a state-issued license, not all states honor this.

When traveling, it is the gun owner's responsibility to know and abide by the gun laws in each state they visit. Even if a state has constitutional carry, it may only apply to that state's residents.

This is why it is important for us as trainers to emphasize the value of continuing to obtain a concealed carry license so firearm owners can continue to conceal carry legally in the states that offer reciprocity and avoid any potential legal headaches.

Grow Your Business by Expanding Your Training Offerings

Attract new students and enhance the learning of existing clients by offering continuing firearm training. Don't just focus on the concealed carry aspect of gun ownership - many people choose to own firearms and never carry them in public. They need information, too.

Draw upon your existing knowledge and skill set to develop additional training opportunities and attract students.

These types of classes likely won't require you to obtain any further instructor "credentials" in order to teach them, meaning you can add training to your roster without spending hundreds or even thousands of dollars for "certified" classes that your market won't be interested in.

Basic additional firearm training, even when not required by law, offers numerous benefits to clients, such as:

Enhanced Safety

- **Accident Prevention:** Regular training reduces the risk of accidental discharges and mishandling of firearms. Teach proper handling and finger and muzzle discipline.

- **Safety Protocols:** Continuous education on the latest safety practices and protocols ensures your student and those around your student remain safe. Cover topics such as proper firearm storage and transport, as well as talking to kids about guns.

Skill Improvement

- **Accuracy and Precision:** Ongoing practice hones your student's shooting accuracy and precision, which is essential for effective self-defense. This can be done via live fire at a range or using airsoft or laser fire guns in a classroom.

- **Advanced Techniques:** Teach and help your student master advanced shooting techniques and tactics that basic training might not cover. Work on drawing from a holster, keeping the finger properly indexed and off the trigger until ready to shoot and how to properly re-holster a firearm. Engaging a target. These can all be done with live fire, if your range allows it, or by using inert training pistols.

Legal Knowledge

- **Updated Laws:** Are there new laws in your state? Keep your students informed about changes in firearm laws and regulations, ensuring compliance and avoiding legal issues. These classes can be done in person or via an online webinar.

- **Self-Defense Laws:** Give a deeper understanding of self-defense laws and the legal use of force. Many gun owners will never carry a firearm in public but may have one in the home for self-defense. They need to know the law too.

- **How to Dial 911** - When does a call start recording? What information to give? What NOT to give? Should they stay on the line? When to call an attorney.

Confidence Building

- **Increased Confidence:** Regular training builds confidence in your student's ability to handle and use their firearm effectively in various situations. The worst thing a student can do is carry a firearm they are not confident in operating, pull that firearm out in a defensive situation, freeze, or have a malfunction. Train.

- **Preparedness:** Help them feel more prepared and capable of defending themselves and others if necessary. What to do and how to do it. Run them through shoot/don't shoot scenarios to help hone decision-making skills.

Situational Awareness

- **Threat Recognition:** Improve your student's ability to recognize and assess potential threats quickly and accurately.

- **Decision-Making:** Enhance your student's decision-making skills under pressure, which is crucial for effective self-defense.

Maintenance of Skills

- **Muscle Memory:** Consistent PROPER training reinforces muscle memory, making your student's actions more instinctive and reliable.

- **Skill Retention:** Encourage additional training to prevent skill degradation over time by regularly practicing and refreshing their training.

Physical and Mental Discipline

- **Focus and Discipline**: Help students improve their focus, discipline, and mental resilience through regular training.

- **Stress Management:** Teach techniques for managing stress and staying calm in high-pressure situations.

If you can think it – you can teach it. Dig deep in your knowledge base and GROW

Webinars & Video-On-Demand

Not every class requires you to deliver it live and in person.

Your ability to provide training via webinars or recorded videos represents a significant advancement in accessibility and convenience for both you and your students.

Webinars allow you to deliver live, interactive sessions that can reach participants regardless of geographical location and the restrictions of finding a classroom to teach in.

This flexibility means that you can engage with a larger audience, breaking down the barriers imposed by physical distances. Participants can join in real-time, ask questions, and engage in discussions, creating a dynamic and collaborative learning environment.

Additionally, webinars can be scheduled at various times to accommodate different time zones, making it easier for participants to attend sessions that fit their schedules.

Recorded video training further enhances the learning experience by offering on-demand access to educational content. This means your students can revisit the material as often as needed, ensuring they fully understand and retain the information.

It also caters to different learning paces and styles, allowing individuals to pause, rewind, and fast-forward through the content as well as to complete the learning on a schedule that is convenient to them.

For you as an instructor, recorded training videos can be a cost-effective solution, as they eliminate the need for repeated live sessions and can be reused over and over.

By adapting a combination of webinars and recorded videos to your training offerings, you create a versatile, scalable, and effective training solution that maximizes both reach and impact.

There may be some restrictions here, as one can imagine.

For example, your State may require in-person training for some classes you teach. This is especially true for classes like Concealed Pistol License training and certification courses.

There are PLENTY of classes where online learning is more than sufficient. One of those classes is a basic Introduction to Handguns course.

Designed for students who are interested in gaining some firearm knowledge BEFORE they take an in-person class.

This 35-Minute Video-On-Demand delivery class means they can watch it on any internet connected device when it is most convenient for them. It's perfect for the person who is not familiar with firearms or firearm vernacular - they then come to a future class prepared to learn, with the basic knowledge any gun owner should have.

I often sell this class for $9.95 - I also give it away FREE to people in the form of a sales funnel - Give me your name and e-mail and you get a free class. I get a hot lead for a potential client.

Case Study - Listen to Your Students

In the state of Michigan, Concealed Pistol License holders are required to RENEW their Michigan CPL license every five years.

☐ Renewal – If renewing an existing Standard license, complete the renewal information and certification below.			
1. Renewal Information			
a. Expiration Date of Current CPL	b. County of Issuance	c. Name on Previous License	d. CPL Number
2. Renewal Certification			
I certify that I have completed at least three hours of review of the required training and have had at least one hour of firing range time in the six months immediately preceding this application.			
Signature			Date

The state requires CPL holders to complete at least three hours of the required training (they don't even say what that is) and have had at least one hour of firing range time in the six months immediately preceding the application for renewal. It does not say you need to take a class. It just says you need at least three hours of review of the required training.

As you can imagine, this created a wealth of phone calls asking if we had a class for this. At the time, we did not. After fielding what were MANY DOZENS of phone calls asking for said renewal class, Jim put down the mandate - "give them what they are asking for "- so we made one.

The state didn't have an actual outline for what they wanted to see as far as curriculum for a renewal class, other than to say "the required training," so we defaulted to the state requirement for training to qualify for a Michigan Concealed Pistol License.

The Detroit Arms 3-Hour Michigan CPL Renewal Class was born! In this three-hour class, we simply review the state requirements for the information that was required to be covered in the initial Michigan Concealed Pistol License Class:

- The safe storage, use, and handling of a pistol includes but is not limited to, safe storage, use, and handling to protect child safety.
- Ammunition knowledge.
- The fundamentals of pistol shooting.
- Pistol shooting positions.
- Firearms law, including civil liability issues & use of deadly force.
- Avoiding criminal attacks and controlling a violent confrontation.
- All laws that apply to carrying a concealed pistol in Michigan.

Before you knew it, we were teaching this class once a week to a full classroom of eager students.

No range time - no outward expense regarding student materials. Just us and a room full of people paying $50.00 to hear us feed them the information they needed.

Then it was...Do you have a book?

"Give them what they ask for" Jim said again, so I took the time to put our class down on paper - converted it to PDF format - and a book was born.

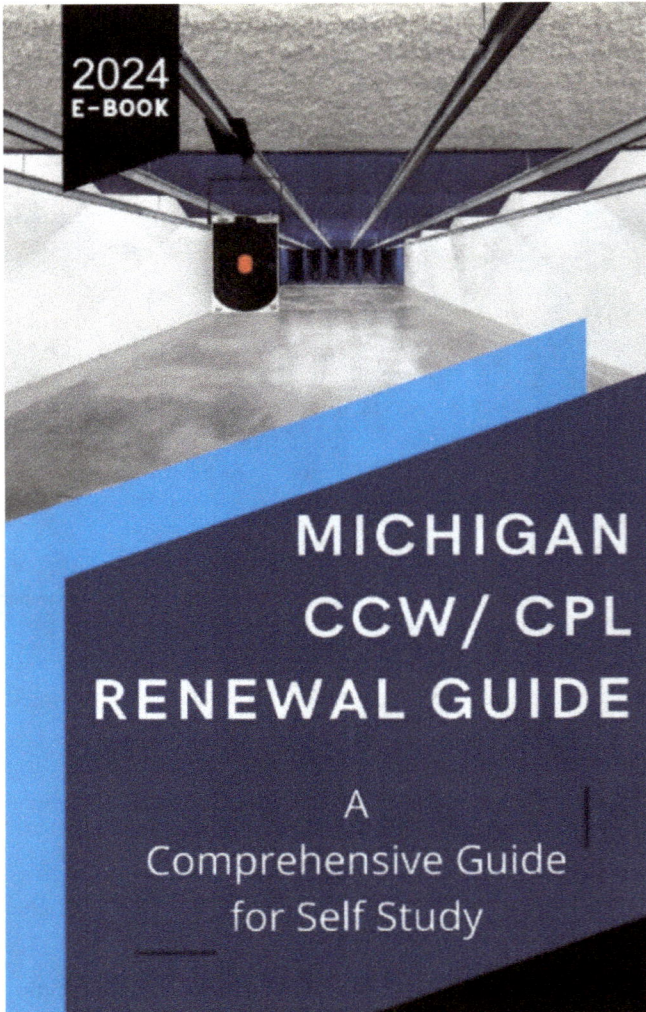

This digital e-book sells for $14.99 online - on the Detroit Arms website - the shopping cart has an auto web-hook that automatically delivers the book to a customer's inbox upon payment. It is available 24/7/365.

Which then became...how about a video?

Into the studio, I went. Just me with my trusty PowerPoint presentation and a good microphone - we took to recording the class for Video on Demand. I was not on camera; I just narrated the slides on the screen.

This video sells for $37.95, students can watch it 24 hours a day, 7 days a week, 365 days a year - when it is convenient for the student. They can watch it in segments or all at once. It became an instant hit. You know what else it did? Took my Renewal Training class from being available in my local area to being offered in the **ENTIRE STATE OF MICHIGAN.**

A New Website is Born...

Michigan Concealed Pistol License Holders

Is it time to renew your CPL?

The state of Michigan requires Michigan CPL renewal applicants to sign an affidavit certifying that they have completed at least three hours of review of the required training and have had at least one hour of firing range time in the six months immediately preceding the submission of a renewal application.

We offer the Michigan CPL Renewal class on our website, but it soon came into question that the name Detroit Arms might not play as well in towns that are hundreds of miles from Detroit.

People over 500 miles away in the Upper Peninsula (like Houghton, Michigan) would see the name Detroit and think "well that can't be for our area" even though the training is valid for all counties in Michigan.

Why not just call the website www.Michigan-CPL-Renewal.com?

And so, it was. This took our ability to successfully offer a class to students all over the state.

How did we market to the entire state?

EASY! I simply joined Facebook groups for cities and towns all over the state of Michigan and began posting ads.

Capturing An Entire State

Instead of driving traffic from just my local community, I'm able to market all over the state to an audience of tens of thousands of people! I belong to hundreds of groups all over the state of Michigan, where I post my ad and gain clients.

Michigan Small Business
Public group · 23.6K members

Dee Hankins ▶ **Michigan Small Business**
June 3 at 8:07 PM ·

Need to RENEW your Michigan CPL? A 3-Hour Review of the required training
https://Michigan-CPL-Renewal.com is required - an actual class is not necessary - we have
everything you should know right here. Valid for ALL counties. Next in person class 6/19
10-1 21 Mile & Gratiot Chesterfield - Online video runs 7 days a week 24 hours a day

You never get a second chance to make a good first impression. – Will Rogers

Customer Service

First impressions count. From the moment a client picks up a phone and dials your number - visits your Google Business Profile or your website - how attentive you were their needs matters and if you don't meet expectations right out of the gate - you've already lost the game.

Customer service is undeniably the cornerstone of a successful business, as that vital first impression sets the tone for a customer's entire experience with you - or lack of it.

The initial interaction a client has with you as a firearm instructor often defines their perception of your brand, making it crucial for you to invest in creating a welcoming, responsive, and helpful atmosphere from the outset.

This first impression is more than a fleeting moment; it is the foundation upon which trust is built. When customers feel valued and understood, they are more likely to develop a sense of loyalty and confidence in your ability as a subject matter expert to meet their needs.

Consistent, high-quality customer service ensures that clients feel supported and appreciated at every touchpoint, reinforcing their decision to work with you. This ongoing trust is not just beneficial for repeat business; it is a powerful driver of referral business as well.

Satisfied customers become brand advocates, sharing their positive experiences with friends, family, and colleagues.

This word-of-mouth promotion is invaluable, as it brings in new clients who are pre-disposed to trust you as a trainer, thanks to the recommendations of their peers.

Plain and simple, exceptional customer service creates a virtuous cycle of satisfaction and growth, propelling the business toward sustained success.

For you as a small business owner, providing exceptional customer service involves several key steps, beginning with the initial phone call and continuing consistently throughout your engagement with your client.

It's not always easy, as for many firearm instructors this is not their full-time job but rather a "side hustle" that they may one day hope to turn into a full time employment opportunity.

EVEN IF it's a side hustle, it still needs to be treated as a legitimate business, mostly because it is! Let's start with some fundamentals of GREAT customer service and build from there.

- **Prompt and Polite Initial Contact:** Answering phone calls quickly and with a courteous greeting sets a positive tone. Use a friendly and professional manner, making sure to introduce yourself and the business.

  If I had a dollar for every instructor I've called who didn't answer the phone, who didn't have voicemail set up, or who had a voicemail box that was full and I couldn't leave a message, I wouldn't be writing this book.

  If you can't answer, make sure you can at least take a message. It goes without saying that you should **RETURN THOSE CALLS** as soon as possible, at the very least the same day. Every missed call is a missed revenue opportunity. Call back every missed call.

This is where the use of automation and technology can set you apart from your competition - we will talk about Missed Call Text Back shortly.

- **Attentive Listening and Understanding:** The customer doesn't know what they don't know, and we can't be effective teachers if we only listen and respond. We need to listen to UNDERSTAND before we respond.

  Show genuine interest in the customer's concerns by listening attentively without interrupting. Ask clarifying questions to ensure you understand their needs and repeat back key points to confirm understanding.

- **Provide Knowledgeable and Helpful Responses:** Provide accurate and relevant information, whether via phone or via your website. Be well-informed and ready to offer solutions or alternatives to anything a customer might throw at you. If you don't have an immediate answer, assure the customer you will find out and follow up promptly.

Many of my callers throughout the day are not even looking for training but rather things like FFL transfers, where to source a decent holster, what government agency to call to find out if they have any felonies on their record (I wish I was kidding), etc. Be able to point them in the proper direction rather than just answering, "I don't know" or "I don't do that."

- **Personalized Service:** Make every attempt to tailor your approach to meet the specific needs of each customer. Use their name during the conversation to create a personal connection. And make them feel valued.

While much of what we do is cookie cutter delivery, need to make them confident they made the right decision by hiring you.

- **Efficient Problem Resolution:** We can't please everyone - we are not pizza. Address any issues or complaints swiftly and effectively. Apologize, if necessary, take responsibility, and offer a clear plan to resolve the problem. Keep the customer updated on the progress and ensure they are satisfied with the resolution.

  How you handle a situation is important, especially if the customer chooses to go public with the information, such as on a Google review. Future customers will make a hiring decision based on how you handled yourself and not always on what occurred in the customer's eyes.

- **Clear Communication:** Maintain transparency throughout the entire sales and training process. Put policies and expectations in writing wherever possible. Clearly explain the next steps, timelines, and any costs involved. Many customers make multiple calls prior to hiring an instructor, which can confuse conversations. Send confirmation e-mails outlining expectations - things like:

  o Date and time of class
  o Location of class and specific directions/landmarks
  o What time should they plan to arrive
    Any items they should bring
    How they should dress
  o Directions for proper transport of a handgun (if needed)
  o Any waivers that need completion before class
  o Cancellation policy
    Contact information for the instructor

- **Follow-Up:** After the initial interaction, follow up with the customer to ensure their needs were met and they are satisfied with the outcome. A simple follow-up call or email can go a long way in showing that you care about their experience.

Upon completion of any class at Detroit Arms, we send a thank you email to each and every client, thanking them for attending class with us and letting them know that if we missed meeting their expectations in any way, we want to know about it so we can correct it.

Not everyone learns at the same pace, and it's possible that the delivery of information was too much for some. It's our job to help them feel whole.

At Detroit Arms, we offer Alumni the ability to attend the classroom portion of any upcoming Concealed Carry class FREE if they bring us a paying client. It's a true win-win for both of us.

- **Consistency and Reliability:** Provide consistent service every time a customer interacts with your business. Reliability builds trust, as customers will know they can count on you to deliver. Studies show that 83% of customers are open to referring a business after having a successful interaction.

There's a reason fast food restaurants have well thought out and executed product prep and delivery standards. In theory the idea is that you get the same meal every time you visit. Consistency breeds growth.

- **Exceeding Expectations:** Go the extra mile for your customers. Small gestures, like providing free bottled water or snacks during a class, can leave a lasting positive impression.

Our Michigan Concealed Pistol License class, for example, is an 8-hour event, per the state of Michigan. We charge just about the same price (give or take $20) as most other instructors in the area. We spend a little more money on the lunch we bring in, the snacks we provide, and the beverages provided.

I also make homemade chocolate chip cookies fresh each morning for class. The students are greeted in the morning with the smell of fresh brewed coffee and cookies before the class even starts. There are little "amenities" throughout the classroom such as comfortable chairs, hand sanitizer, tissues, ladies' sanitary needs in the bathroom, flavored drink mixes for in the water, a variety of coffee creamers.

Little touches that don't cost much but show we care about their comfort throughout the day. If you look at our reviews, you'll see that cookies are mentioned a lot. They are the little things that make an impression and carry over to customer satisfaction.

Referrals

Any savvy business owner will tell you that referrals are a **goldmine** for sustainable growth. Referral business leverages the power of satisfied customers who then become ambassadors for your brand, spreading positive word-of-mouth within their networks of friends and family.

This organic form of marketing is not only highly effective but also cost-efficient. Unlike traditional advertising, which can be expensive and uncertain in terms of return on investment, referrals come with built-in trust.

When a friend, family member, or colleague recommends a business, it carries a level of credibility that paid ads struggle to match. This pre-established trust means potential clients are more inclined to engage with the business, accelerating the conversion process and fostering long-term loyalty.

New customers who are referred to you by someone they trust are not only more likely to choose your business but also tend to have a higher lifetime value.

These clients arrive with a positive impression, reducing the effort needed to close the sale and increasing the likelihood of repeat business.

This cycle of satisfaction and referral creates a self-sustaining engine of growth, making it a cornerstone strategy for any savvy business owner aiming for lasting success.

If you could only get new clients from referrals, what would your product/service delivery look like?
- Alex Hormozi

To effectively generate referral business from your customers, you should:

- **Provide Exceptional Service:** Ensure that you consistently exceed your customers' expectations. Satisfied customers are more likely to share their positive experiences with others, becoming natural advocates for you, bringing you clients.

- **Ask for Referrals:** Directly request referrals from happy customers. Many customers are willing to help but might need a little prompting - give them an easy-to-use link to your Google Business Profile page in your thank you e-mail!

- **Create a Referral Program:** Reward customers for bringing in new business. Offer incentives such as special discounts for their friends and family or exclusive access to new classes (online classes are perfect for this!). Make it easy for customers to refer you by providing them with referral cards, links, or codes they can share.

At Detroit Arms we offer Alumni the ability to return to our Michigan Concealed Carry Class FREE with a paying client - no matter how long it's been since they took a class - as long as they bring us a paying client, they get to attend the classroom portion again free. It's a win-win for both of us!

- **Leverage social media:** Encourage your customers to share their experiences on social media. Run contests or campaigns where customers can win prizes for posting about your business and tagging you. Highlight these posts on your own social media channels to show appreciation.

- **Provide Excellent Post-Sale Support:** Ensure your customers feel supported even after they've attended a class or training with you. Follow up with them to see how they are and if they need any further assistance, even if it's just via e-mail. Happy, well-supported customers are more likely to refer others.

Don't Fall Victim to Price Wars

I see it in nearly every market, including our own. Some hot shot instructor is going to set the world on fire and dominate the market by slashing the price of their class in order to encourage people to attend their training.

In areas such as the metropolitan Detroit market, where the typical pricing is $100.00 - $150.00+ per student for an 8-hour class, these instructors open up shop and offer $50.00 or even FREE classes.

This not only disrupts everyone else's business in the market, but it is not a sustainable long-term plan for the instructor who is doing it.

Furthermore, it does not attract what we term the "optimal customer." People who shop for training based on a lowball price alone are one-time wonders. They don't tend to become repeat clients, and all their referrals are looking for a cheap deal as well.

Pitfalls of Competing in a Pricing War

- **Eroded Profit Margins:** Lowering prices to compete can drastically reduce profit margins. For the instructor doing this, it can make it difficult to cover operational costs and invest in quality help, equipment, or improvements.

- **Perceived Value:** Consistently low prices may lead customers to perceive your services as low quality. This can tarnish your reputation and make it difficult to attract customers who value high-quality training. Know your worth!

- **Unsustainable Business Model:** Competing on price alone is not a sustainable business model. Larger competitors with more resources can outlast you in a pricing war, eventually driving you out of the market. We've experienced this with local gun ranges in our market who are lowballing their class for "door swings" as they want to bait people in for the cheap training with the hope of selling them guns.

- **Attracting the Wrong Clientele:** Price-sensitive customers who choose your services solely based on cost are less likely to be loyal. They are more likely to switch to a competitor as soon as a lower price is available, leading to high customer churn rates. Plus, all of their potential referral customers will also be shopping that lowball price. It's a never-ending cycle.

- **Difficulty Raising Prices:** Once you've established a low price point, raising prices can be challenging. Even if your class is a better-quality experience and worth a few extra bucks, customers accustomed to paying less may resist price increases, leading to potential loss of business in the long run.

Strategies to Avoid the Lowball Pricing Trap

- **Differentiate on Quality and Value:** Emphasize the quality of your training programs, your expertise, and the success rates of your students. Highlight unique selling points such as personalized training plans, safety protocols, and post-training support.

- **Build a Strong Brand:** Develop a strong brand identity that communicates the value and quality of your services. Invest in professional-looking marketing materials, a user-friendly website, and an active social media presence to build trust and credibility.

- **Focus on Customer Experience:** Provide an exceptional customer experience from the first point of contact to post-training follow-up. Amazing customer service, comfortable facilities, and responsive communication can differentiate you from competitors who focus solely on price.

- **Leverage Testimonials and Reviews:** Encourage satisfied clients to leave positive reviews and testimonials. Real-life success stories and endorsements can significantly influence potential customers and justify prices higher than your competition.

- **Educate Your Customers:** Educate potential clients about the risks of choosing low-cost, low-quality training. Use blog posts, videos, and informational sessions to explain the importance of proper training, safety, and the long-term benefits of investing in quality instruction.

Instead of focusing on price, prioritize quality, the overall customer experience, and strong brand positioning. By differentiating your services and emphasizing value, you can attract the right clientele who appreciate the importance of high-quality training and are willing to pay a premium for it.

"Talent wins games, but teamwork and intelligence win championships."
- Michael Jordan

11 USING AUTOMATION

A CRM Program Can Help!

Client Management

- **Centralized Database:** All your client information is stored in one place, including contact details, training history, preferences, and feedback. This includes any contact they've made with you via chat on social media platforms and your website; no more scrolling and overlooking who contacted you and where - it's all in one place.

- **Segmentation:** You can categorize clients based on their training level, interests, or other relevant criteria, enabling targeted communication and personalized service.

Scheduling and Appointments

- **Automated Scheduling:** Students can book training sessions online, reducing administrative workload and ensuring efficient time management.

- **Reminders:** You can send automated reminders to clients about upcoming classes, reducing no-shows and ensuring clients are prepared.

Marketing and Communication

- **Email Campaigns:** Design and send marketing emails to your clients.

- **SMS/Text Messaging:** Communicate important information or reminders directly to clients' phones, ensuring timely and direct engagement. The open rate of SMS messages is 98% vs. 28% with a traditional email and a read rate of 42%.

- **Social Media Integration:** One click posting to Facebook, Instagram and more! Schedule your posts days, weeks or even months in advance!

- **Missed Call Text Back:** Even if a potential customer doesn't leave a message when they call and hang up, they get a personalized message FROM YOU starting a dialogue.

- **Webchat!** Increase website conversions with an on-site chat - it's an absolute game-changer. I book students every day via chat!

Lead Generation and Sales

- **Lead Capture:** Use landing pages, forms, and funnels to capture potential client information and convert leads into paying customers. Imagine launching a FREE ad on a platform such as Facebook and having interested individuals give you their name and email address to receive information from you. There's no hotter lead out there!

- **Sales Pipeline:** Track potential clients through different stages of the sales process, from initial contact to closing the deal. Never forget where you were in the process.

- **Follow-Up Automation:** Set up automated follow-ups for leads, ensuring no opportunity is missed. Keep in front of your clients every step of the way.

Payment

- **Payment Processing:** Integrate with payment gateways such as Stripe to accept payments online, simplifying financial transactions.

Business & Class Management

- **Websites:** Our CRM offers website hosting with an included drag-and-drop editor and themes we provide to make creating and launching a site quick and easy!

- **Course Listings:** Manage and display available classes, workshops, and events.

- **Online Learning Platform:** Create and host your own video e-learning courses.

- **Registration:** Allow clients to register and pay for classes online.

Analytics and Reporting

- **Performance Metrics:** Track key performance indicators such as client acquisition, retention rates, and revenue.

- **Client Insights:** Analyze client behavior and preferences to tailor services and improve client satisfaction.

Workflow Automation

- **Task Management:** Automate routine tasks, such as sending welcome emails to new clients, reminder emails to students who have registered for training, or follow-up messages to clients sent after training sessions. All done automatically!

- **Custom Workflows:** Create customized workflows to streamline business processes and ensure consistency in client interactions. Imagine being able to re-target clients for additional training without having to remember what previous class they took and when, and then remember to send an email yourself. The CRM does it for you!

Reputation Management Tools

- **Google Reviews:** Get client reviews automatically! Never forget to ask for a review - the system will send out the request to you.

- **Direct Reporting:** Your customer reviews are automatically posted to Google - and you can respond to reviews and share them automatically!

Mobile App

- **IOS & Android Compatible:** Provides two-way communication with clients and potential students on any device - right in the palm of your hand! You don't need to be in front of a computer to operate your business - you can do it from your cell phone!

Unlimited Team Members

- Anyone you choose, anywhere they are. Delegate tasks when you're not available.

By integrating a CRM system into your operation, you can enhance efficiency, improve client engagement, and streamline administrative tasks, allowing you to focus more on money-making activities and growing your business.

Does Detroit Arms use a CRM?

We most certainly do! You might think - "A CRM sounds intimidating. I don't have time to learn any new programs." I could ask you if you have time to work twice as hard at obtaining customers. Why stop income-generating activities when you can automate them?

By utilizing the automation services of a CRM, I can stay on top of the menial tasks that would otherwise consume my day.

How so? Well, I'm going to let you in on a little secret. (This is Doreen speaking) I do 99% of all the tasks for Detroit Arms as one person. I'm the person responsible for:

- Answering the phone
- Answering the chats
- Answering the email
- Answering the front door
- Scheduling the classes
- Marketing the classes
- Reminding the students about the classes
- Creating all the kits/printed materials for class
- Setting up the classroom
- Baking the cookies
- Making the coffee
- Greeting the students
- Teaching / Hosting the classes
- I'm the Lunch Lady
- Cleaning the facility after the classes
- Following up with the students after the classes
- Rinse and repeat

In other words, I do it all.

Jim is here in support - he even shares in the teaching of the classes - but for the most part, the responsibility for keeping all the balls in the air falls directly on me.

This is my classroom. I'm responsible for putting butts in those seats.

We teach the Michigan Concealed Carry class several times a month. (Our schedule is slower in the summer and weekly in the fall/winter)

I routinely put 20-40 butts in seats for every single class **WITHOUT** any paid advertising.

HOW?

It begins with utilizing a CRM (Customer Relationship Management Software) and Automation.

- **Client Management** - With CRM, I can maintain a central database of all my clients, past and present. I have all their contact information easily accessible. By having this information contained in one spot, I'm able to refer to past conversations and include them in targeted email campaigns or SMS/Text campaigns.

- **Automated Scheduling** - Customers can book classes direct from my website. It doesn't require a phone call between me and the customer in order to book them into a class. When a customer books off the link on my website, it automatically puts their information into my CRM - I don't have to duplicate the effort by adding them into a spreadsheet or other method of keeping track of names, addresses and phone numbers.

- **Marketing & Communication** - This is the good part. So much of what I am tasked with doing daily when it comes to Customer Service is able to be automated.

I've said it before, and I'm going to say it again - You never get a second chance to make a great first impression.

Everything you do to build and grow your business will be a result of marketing and communication.

- **Missed Call Text Back** - As you can imagine, my phone can get pretty busy. When a potential client opens the Google Machine and types in "gun classes near me," they get a list of about 20 businesses in the vicinity. When they call me, and I don't answer, what do they do? They hang up and call the next person on the list.

With Missed Call Text Back - **EVEN IF THEY DON'T LEAVE A MESSAGE** - they get an automated text message immediately delivered to their phone from me thanking them for calling and telling them I will be with them momentarily.

GAME CHANGER. This inserts an automatic pause, and I'm able to capture the client before they call someone else.

- **Webchat** - If you're not offering chat as a means of communication, you are truly missing out. You would be surprised at the number of text messages I field throughout the course of a day that turn into booked business.

WHY? People love to chat vs. call on the phone. It's anonymous - it stops the person in the cubicle next to them from knowing what they are calling about on the phone - it's truly a preferred method of communication for many.

I offer the ability to chat on my website and on my Facebook page. I also offered it on my Google Business Profile, but Google is discontinuing that service in July of 2024.

- **SMS/Texting** - I have the ability to communicate to students via SMS/Text in the event I want to send out a mass message. Customers can opt-in/out of receiving SMS messages. It could be as simple as a "flash sale" that I'm running, a special event I wish to promote or even an emergency message relevant to my students. The open rate of SMS messages is 98% vs. 28% with a traditional email.

- **E-Mail** - Why stay in touch with your past clients? They're the best source of referrals! Keeping your relationships with past clients active is a terrific source of referral business. If your relationship ends at the end of class, you run the risk of leaving your clients' minds. When you maintain the relationship, though, you ensure your clients will remember you AND REFER YOU!

DID YOU KNOW it costs 6-7x less money to market to an existing client than it does to market to and gain a new one? Studies show that 83% of customers are open to referring a business after conducting a successful purchase. Referred customers are four times more likely to refer others to the same business. Stay in touch with your clients. I'm able to design and send email campaigns right from the CRM.

- **Social media** - Imagine being able to send out a marketing message across all of your social media accounts with the click of one button. The CRM integrates with all my social accounts - Facebook Twitter, TikTok, etc. I create a marketing message once and with one click can have it posted across all platforms.

Plus I can schedule messages out a week, a month or even a YEAR of activities all at once, and can even schedule multiple messages a day.

It allows me to add to - or delete - ads at any time. No more "forgetting" to keep your audience engaged - my ads and messages post automatically on the dates and times I choose.

Being able to plan out weeks in advance and use my messaging helps keep the momentum flowing as I try to encourage students to sign up for class. Due to Facebook restrictions, it does NOT post into Facebook groups - those I do manually.

- **Lead Capture** - I use landing pages, forms, and funnels to capture potential client information and convert leads into paying customers. I simply put a free ad on a platform such as Facebook offering **"FREE INFORMATION,"** like my online Introduction to Handguns class, or a downloadable guide I create like "10 Things Every Firearm Owners Should Know," etc. Interested individuals, click the link I provide and provide their name and email address so I can receive information. There's no hotter lead out there!

- **Sales Pipeline** - Once a potential client enters their information and receives the information I have offered, I then can track them through the different stages of the sales process, from initial contact to closing the deal.

- **Follow-Up Automation:** I can set up automated follow-ups for leads, ensuring no opportunity is missed. Keep in front of your clients every step of the way. If I reach out to them and they say "Oh, call me back next month" I'm able to tag their file for automatic follow up next month.

- **Payment Processing:** I'm able to integrate my website with payment gateways such as Stripe to accept payments online, simplifying financial transactions.

- **Websites:** Our CRM offers website hosting with an included drag-and-drop editor and themes we provide to make creating and launching a site quick and easy! I manage the Detroit Arms website right from the CRM platform and can make changes quickly and easily without having any coding knowledge.

- **Online Learning Platform:** I'm able to create and host my own video e-learning courses. You say "well, I can do that on YouTube and monetize it" or "there are plenty of other places I can host training". **You're not wrong.**

HOWEVER - YouTube requires you to have thousands of viewers to monetize your class, and then you get paid about 10 cents per view. Not a huge money maker.

Other class platforms are NOT necessarily 2A friendly, and they take a percentage of your overall sales for any videos you produce and sell. This is not the case here.

I'm able to create courses, charge for them, and keep 100% of the money generated, with well fewer credit card fees. It's a total game-changer. I don't monetize every video I put up; I have the ability to decide.

Either way, having the ability to record and offer video on demand training 24/7/365 means I can make money while I sleep.

Some of the self-created Video-On-Demand courses I offer are:

Real Estate Agent Safety

Safety Tips & Techniques for the Real Estate Professional

2-Hour Online Class

Real Estate Agents face unique risks, unlike those in other professions, simply due to the nature of the job. Prepare yourself with strategies to keep both you and your clients safe.

Join us to discuss the finer points of tuning into your environment through situational awareness, helping you avoid a potentially violent encounter.

Learn How to Identify Risks   **Learn Self Defense Strategies**   **Develop A Plan**

On-Demand Video Course - Watch At Your Convenience

Practical Self Defense

Safety Tips & Techniques for ANYONE looking to increase safety

- **Task Management:** I can automate routine tasks, such as sending welcome emails to new clients, reminder emails to students who have registered for training, or follow-up messages to clients sent after training sessions. All done automatically!

- **Reputation Management** - Google Reviews: Get client reviews automatically! Never forget to ask for a review - the system sends out the request automatically on a schedule I pre-determine.

Class Scheduling Software / Services

Choosing the scheduling system that your customers will use to select your class is critical.

There are so many different offerings out there that claim to solve this problem but, you will eventually find that you'll want something more, and perhaps at some point you could be left having to migrate from what you initially chose.

I'll try to characterize the two high-level choices to start with.

Marketplace

Marketplaces are common, and are either provided by the firearms training organization, like the USCCA or NRA or hosted as a service by a third party.

The chief advantage to these is speed adoption. In minutes, you can have your site up and running to list your classes and then drive traffic to these pages in the hopes you get the sign-ups.

There are significant differences between the ones provided for free or low-cost vs commercial offerings as it relates to features. That is something you will want to consider.

Usually, the free ones are light on features, especially in relation to things like rescheduling and customer communications, which are normally non-existent.

Why would you want to be able to do this via the service?

Your time and customer experience. Nobody likes a reschedule but, it happens. So, if we can make this process more streamlined it takes some of the pain out of it for you and more importantly for your customer, who is a referral source for you for future business.

Like it or not, the customer experience extends outside of the time they spend with you in class. It's also about the entire experience from ease of scheduling, plain and fair and easy to use rescheduling etc. It matters.

Downsides to marketplaces is they do tend to commoditize your offer by throwing you in a list where users will shop the bazaar of other instructors.

Most marketplaces have a stagnant set of features. What you see today is likely what's going to be there a year from now. Your mileage may vary.

Self-Hosted Branded

If you really want to roll your sleeves up, you could host your own scheduling system.

There are various offerings, including WordPress plugins, that, when combined with some customizations and required integrations with many other plugins for e-commerce, e-mail, CRM, etc., can cobble together your "solution."

I will say we've had some experience doing this with mixed results.

The chief challenge with building atop WordPress is…. WordPress and all the plugins are shifting sand. Each component has its own update and release cycle.

You now own the care and feeding of that system, and the worst part is you troubleshooting it when one of the frequent updates breaks things. When it's broken, so is your sign-up process.

So, everything stops, including you, as you (or your designated person) have to fix it…and **FAST**.

Unbranded Ticketing Systems

There are several unbranded ticketing systems on the market that are designed to facilitate selling tickets to events.

It's a mixed bag out there, with most being really designed for in-person, live events. Most don't white-label custom domain names, but some will offer a little branding, such as logos.

How they charge for their service varies from free for free events to percentage of sale along with flat monthly fees.

They generally will have very basic communications capabilities with the customer such as just the delivery of the ticket and some will have integrations with other software to signal when the purchase happens.

Rescheduling capabilities seem practically non-existent for these types of products.

Also, keep in mind that some of these ticketing system companies have terms of use that occasionally create issues where a firearms instructor gets deplatformed.

It's something we all face, and we have to be able to adapt and overcome as the political and social winds blow, which are mostly not in our favor.

Branded Hosted

This is a blend of the two.

In this case, you have a branded site with your domain that is either your entire site or often the scheduling portion of your site, and your main site links to it.

In this case you have the advantage of having your custom brand and you are exchanging fees to the provider to manage the upkeep of the software.

All you must do is manage the data side of things, such as creating classes, managing student rosters, and the like.

This is particularly attractive to those who want to (and arguably should) focus on the core business of training and let someone else keep the software running.

These services boil down to the cost/benefit analysis of the individual service as it relates to your business, such as firearms training.

We believe this offers the best choice for most firearms instructors, having tried all these different flavors over the years and created agencies in support of firearms instructors.

We've seen both sides of this fence.

In our 16 years of doing business, our experience has shown that some features are critical.

- The system must support branding with your domain name.
- It must support friendly URLs for key features like http://classes.ourdomain.com/calendar
- It must support tracking seating capacity
- It must support rescheduling requests and approvals or auto-approvals
- It must support rescheduling rules, like no sooner than 48 hours before the event
- It must support Stripe - We have found Stripe has one of the best integrations for third-party services
- It must support manual bookings - As an instructor, you will have phone-in orders or group orders taken offline
- It must support group pricing
- It must support discount codes
- It must support cancellation and refunds
- It must notify and remind students of their upcoming classes
- It must support rescheduling an entire class to a different day
- It must support exporting the class roster as CSV for import in other reporting systems like USCCA/NRA
- It must allow students to log in, view their upcoming classes, and access course links, directions, and materials.
- It must support multiple instructors.
- It must support sharing events with others. We call it (DoubleTap Referrals™)
- Ideally, it supports virtual as well as in-person and e-learning courses.
- Must support FAQs Area Managed by Instructor
- Must support customer-to-instructor communication
- It must be 2nd Amendment friendly. (Some sites have been known to cut off service to firearms instructors)

As such, likely by the time you're reading this, our very own service will be available, or will be very soon, to firearms instructors like you!

"Alone we can do so little; together we can do so much." - Helen Keller.

12 COACHING

As a firearms trainer, leveraging the expertise of another instructor for coaching in the setup or development of your business can offer substantial benefits.

First, it provides you with fresh perspectives and proven strategies that you might not have considered. An experienced instructor who has successfully built and managed their own training business can offer invaluable insights into best practices, marketing tactics, customer retention, and operational efficiency.

Plus, finding a coach or mentor can significantly shorten your learning curve, helping you avoid common pitfalls and adopt effective methods more quickly.

The knowledge gained from a seasoned professional can translate into more streamlined operations and higher client satisfaction, ultimately leading to increased profitability for you.

You Don't Know What You Don't Know!

Receiving coaching is not a sign of weakness but rather a strategic decision to enhance your skills, perspectives, and the overall success of your business. Good coaching can help you:

- **Gain Strategic Perspective:** Get an external perspective on your business, offering insights and strategies that you might not have considered.

- **Accountability and Focus:** We help provide accountability, helping you stay focused on your priorities and commitments - things like income producing activities!

- **Skill Development:** At Detroit Arms, we have 16+ years of expertise as trainers and can provide guidance and tools to help you become more effective in running your business.

- **Problem Solving and Decision Making:** When faced with challenges or tough decisions, we can serve as a sounding board, offering constructive feedback and helping you brainstorm solutions. Our experience can be invaluable in navigating obstacles.

- **Personal Growth:** Running a small business is hard. We can support your personal growth, helping you manage stress, build resilience, and succeed!

- **Boost Confidence:** Running a business can sometimes feel overwhelming. We can provide direction, boost your confidence, and inspire you to meet your goals.

- **Long-term Success:** Ultimately, coaching is an investment in the long-term success and sustainability of your business.

We Offer Coaching!!

Our coaching sessions involve not only business strategies but also marketing refinement and enhanced teaching methodologies, ensuring that your training program is attractive and effective for your clients.

By improving and expanding your marketing, branding, and class offerings, you can deliver more engaging and impactful training, which can lead to higher client satisfaction and better word-of-mouth referrals.

Additionally, having an experienced coach provides support and motivation. Running a firearm training business can be challenging, and having someone who understands the intricacies of the firearms training industry (been there - done that) can be reassuring.

As a coach, we can offer encouragement, share our own experiences of overcoming obstacles, and help them maintain a positive outlook. This support system can be crucial in maintaining your enthusiasm, resilience, and focus, which are key to sustaining long-term success.

Moreover, working with another instructor can introduce you to innovative business models and emerging trends. This exposure can inspire you to diversify your services, such as incorporating online or virtual training options.

Diversification not only attracts a broader client base but also creates multiple revenue streams, enhancing your business's stability and growth potential.

Imagine making money while you sleep with 24/7 Video on Demand! Putting more butts in seats than ever before! We do; you can, too! We can help.

Join our Pew Pros coaching program at https://coaching.PewPros.com.

13 CONCLUSIONS

Building and growing a firearms instruction business is a challenging yet rewarding endeavor.

By leveraging the strategies outlined in this guide—ranging from effective marketing to customer relationship management—you have the tools to create a thriving business that stands the test of time.

Remember, success is a journey, not a destination.

Stay committed to your passion, continuously seek improvement, and remain adaptable to the ever-changing landscape of the firearms industry.

Your dedication to excellence and service will not only set you apart but also make a lasting impact on your clients and the broader community.

Thank you for embarking on this journey with us.

Please feel free to reach out to us directly:

https://PewPros.com for Instructor Scheduling Software and More

https://coaching.PewPros.com for Coaching and Marketing Assistance

https://cloudbedrock.com for Custom Software Development Services and CRM offerings

www.ingramcontent.com/pod-product-compliance
Lightning Source LLC
Chambersburg PA
CBHW061257220326
41599CB00028B/5688